INTRODUCTION

Liveries can be an emotive subject, their primary purpose being to promote the corporate image of an organisation with the secondary requirement of being easy to keep looking good and well-maintained.

In the case of a new business the choice of a livery does not have any historical constraints or influences but for a business that is an amalgamation of others, choosing something that neither offends any of the constituent parts nor leans too much towards any one of them, can be quite daunting. This was the situation that faced the British Railways Executive on January 1, 1948 with the amalgamation and Nationalisation of Britain's 'Big Four' railway companies - the Great Western, London Midland, Southern and London & North Eastern Railways - along with a small number of other lines that had escaped the grouping in 1923.

Some enthusiasts hold very strong views about liveries with many remembering with particular fondness those that were in use in their youth, which was the formative time of their interest in railways, with today's heritage lines coming under fire for turning out locomotives in what the individual deems to be the 'wrong' livery. Likewise, those whose passion is to model the railway scene have the challenge of getting everything historically accurate and the locomotive livery is a key part of that.

In the following pages we set out to illustrate the liveries carried by the British Railways steam fleet from 1948 until condemnation, which as you will see, is not as simple as it would at first appear, given that the vast majority of the fleet carried only black or green based liveries throughout the period. To that end the definition of a livery here is any paint, symbol, lettering or number applied to the normally visible part of a locomotive or tender. While British Railways set out detailed specifications for liveries, practicality and human interpretation of the rules led to hundreds of variations to the extent that those wishing to paint either a restored or model locomotive need to ensure that they have access to appropriately dated contemporary photographs of the specific engine to stand a good chance of getting it right!

Via illustrations, the full story of the BR liveries and their variations will unfold but a brief summary of the background may be helpful in putting these into context.

The 1947 Transport Act created the British Transport Commission of which the Railway Executive was a part, this having responsibility for the running of the railways. The act also covered executives for running buses, road transport and the docks among others. The newly formed British Railways had six regions and while five of them reflected the Big Four (the North Eastern Region simply being the old LNER territory from north of Doncaster to the Scottish border) the Scottish Region was an amalgamation of the former LMS and LNER interests in that country. However, at the outset the regions were supposed not to have any influence over such things as corporate liveries.

BR inherited more than 20,000 steam locomotives, many in a run-down state as full recovery from the ravages of World War II was still a long way off. Naturally these locomotives carried the liveries of their former owners, with many being black in either lined or unlined form although in many cases the passengers could not tell that due to the layer of grime that covered many engines. However, the GWR, SR and LNER had started to return mainly express passenger types to their respective shades of green with the LNER even re-instating Garter blue for its A4 Pacifics. The LMS was alone in adopting lined black for its express fleet.

Initially the inherited livery colours were retained for ex-works locomotives but instead of the previous owners' lettering 'British Railways' was applied in a pre 1948 style but loco numbers were prefixed with W, S, M or E depending on their former owner. Very quickly BR introduced the well-known numbering scheme and dictated that 'British Railways' should always appear using the Gill Sans font. Once the new numbering scheme was announced engines were renumbered 'as and when available' but quite often without the former ownership lettering the most powerful passenger types were to be painted blue, with others in a shade of green closely aligned to that of the GWR. Mixed traffic types were to receive lined black and freight engines plain black. The Transport Commission commissioned the design of a 'heraldic device' for each of its divisions with BR getting the well known Lion & Wheel emblem which started to appear in 1949. Subsequently the blue livery was discontinued due to its poor wear capability.

Nothing is new and in 1953 politics intervened on the railway scene again when the Conservatives abolished the various executives, which on the railways resulted in the regions being given more power and influence, particularly over marketing matters which included to some extent liveries and at the same time a new 'heraldic device' was introduced in 1956 to replace the Lion & Wheel, affectionately or otherwise referred to as the 'ferret and dartboard'. The regional freedom on liveries saw many more green engines on the Western and 'red' Pacifics reappear on the Midland. With finances tight and the end of steam in sight the final years of steam engine overhauls saw the introduction of 'economy' liveries, i.e. unlined green or black. The final twist in the liveries tale came with the introduction of BR blue although the only place that it had an impact on our livery story was on the Vale of Rheidol line. ■

Nothing about liveries is predictable - an apparent but totally non-operational pairing of an unlined green tender for a BR Standard Class 2MT with lined green Hall 6953 **Leighton Hall** *at Swindon works on March 26, 1961. A livery variation not seen later is the application of a red stripe to the black axle box covers on the tender.* **T Owen**

CONTENTS

LOCOMOTIVE POWER CLASSIFICATIONS

British Railways developed a power classification system for its locomotives based on a complex formula that took into consideration free gas area, grate area and starting tractive effort with a different version of the formula being used depending on if the engine was intended for passenger or freight duties. This resulted in passenger classifications between 0 and 8 and freight classifications between 0 and 9 with the higher numbers being the more powerful.

So that the power classification was clear to staff it was shown on the cabside of most engines in the form e.g. 8P for a class 8 passenger engine or 7F for a class 7 freight type. Because the formulae gave different figures for passenger and freight work it was possible to have a class designated as e.g. 4P/5F but where the passenger and freight calculations came out at similar levels classes were designated as e.g. 5MT for mixed traffic, so equally suitable for freight and passenger duty. On occasions the latter was then simply shortened to '5'. The Southern Region also added additional letters on occasions.

Although shown in some publications with the BR classification, the Western Region stuck with its own system which used a letter from A-E, instead of a number, with E being the most powerful, the letter being painted on the cabside route disc. However, there were two categories in addition - 'Special' which just applied to the King class and 'Ungrouped' for engines having a tractive effort below 16,500 lb, in both cases there being no letter shown on the cabside. ■

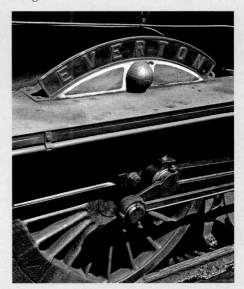

ABOVE: *Jubilee 45572 Eire stands outside Crewe works alongside Stanier Black 5 45499. The Jubilee is freshly painted in lined green whilst 45499 is being prepared for the work. The latter engine is in lined black but carries large cabside numbers, an indication that it may well have received a previous repaint in Scotland, indeed it was allocated to St Rollox at the time of this picture. Unusually the power classification of '5' is painted below the running number whilst that of the Jubilee '6P' is correctly placed above it.*

RIGHT: *The intricacies of liveries and the application of lining can be seen here, these being of interest to the modeller. Firstly we have the painted panel beneath the nameplate of B17/4 61663 Everton as it represents the football club colours, along with the weathering of the orange lining which appears to be absent near bolt fixings but is almost certainly hidden behind the dirt that accumulated in such locations, defying removal by the quick wipe with the cleaning rag.* T OWEN

Editor: Paul Chancellor
Senior Editor: Roger Mortimer
Chief Publishing Officer: Jonathan Jackson
Design: Matt Chapman **Cover:** Lee Howson

Advertising Sales Manager: Brodie Baxter
Email: brodie.baxter@keypublishing.com
Tel: 01780 755131

Advertising Production: Rebecca Antoniades
Email: rebecca.antoniades@keypublishing.com

SUBSCRIPTION/MAIL ORDER
Key Publishing Ltd, PO Box 300,
Stamford, Lincs, PE9 1NA
Tel: 01780 480404 **Fax:** 01780 757812
Subscriptions email: subs@keypublishing.com

Mail Order email: orders@keypublishing.com
Website: www.keypublishing.com/shop

PUBLISHING
Group CEO and Publisher: Adrian Cox
Chief Content & Commercial Officer: Mark Elliott
Head of Customer Engagement:
Gaynor Hemmingway-Gibbs

Key Publishing Ltd, PO Box 100, Stamford, Lincs, PE9 1XP
Tel: 01780 755131 **Website:** www.keypublishing.com

PRINTING
Precision Colour Printing Ltd, Telford,
Shropshire. TF7 4QQ

DISTRIBUTION
Seymour Distribution Ltd, 2 Poultry Avenue,
London, EC1A 9PU **Enquiries Line:** 02074 294000.

LIVERIES OF THE BIG FOUR

Before beginning our trip through post-Nationalisation liveries we will take a brief look at those in use immediately before the formation of British Railways. It has to be kept in mind that, whilst some attempt had been made to restore front line motive power to its pre war splendour, there was a vast backlog of work to catch up on and black and often dirty engines were the norm. On the Great Western Railway green had always been the dominant colour so the extensive use of black during the war years was clearly a retrograde step. After the war the company tried to bring back green extensively and changed the company lettering style to GW with the coat of arms placed centrally on passenger engines but just used the letters GWR on freight types. Similarly the Southern Railway promoted Malachite green extensively and the norm was to use what was termed 'sunshine lettering' throughout. The LMS decided that black, either lined or plain, was the way to go and yet some red painted engines remained and the LNER re-instated Garter Blue on its A4s and Apple green for many other classes with only the true freight workhorses receiving black livery. ■

Pride of the Great Western Railway, King 6000 **King George V** *arrives at Reading in April 1947 in its full green attire with the GW lettering with crest on the tender. The engine number was always carried on the buffer beam.* **P HUGHES**

Dean Goods 2460 was typical of the locomotives painted black, carrying GWR on the tender and is seen at Severn Tunnel Junction in May 1947. **P HUGHES**

The Merchant Navy Pacifics were the front line motive power on the Southern Railway but due to their shape did not follow tradition when it came to livery application. They also had numbers that denoted their wheel arrangement. Showing these features is 21C12 United States Line, (later BR 35012) at Nine Elms in May 1947. Note the red backed nameplate. **P HUGHES**

More typical of Southern Malachite green engines was Schools 922 Marlborough. Although the picture is dated 1948 no livery change had been made at that time.

Denoting better times on the railway and showing how a black engine looked prior to Oliver Bulleid's introduction of new liveries, we see C class 1268 at Ashford in 1937. Some engines made it to Nationalisation still so adorned under the grime. **J P MULLET**

Showing that LMS red survived and did so well into the BR era, is Jubilee 5594 **Bhopal** *seen approaching York in 1949. The engine had been specially repainted for an exhibition held on March 28, 1946 and was very much the exception to the all pervading black used on most LMS engines.* **E SANDERSON**

LEFT: *The LNER provided the most livery variety prior to January 1948. In work worn condition we see A4 11* **Empire of India** *showing off its Garter blue at Newcastle in August 1947. All the constituent railways except the LMS used a painted number at buffer level although in some cases it was difficult to discern through the dirt.* P HUGHES

RIGHT: *Accompanying it at March that day was War Department 73783 in a nice shade of khaki. Many WDs were on loan to the four companies and the LNER even purchased 200 of them. They appeared in various guises but few as clean as this engine! It might have been expected that this example would be one of the 200 that went to the LNER, but it is a 2-10-0 and they all ended up in Scotland with this one becoming 90759.* P HUGHES

The British Railways Steam Years From 1948

*The B1s were in the process of being built in the run up to Nationalisation and did not have to shake off any wartime gloom entering service in pristine Apple green. 1018 **Gnu** is seen at York in 1947. Note the shed allocation painted above the number. C HERBERT*

As previously mentioned, the majority of LMS engines carried black, mostly unlined, in this case worn by a former Furness Railway 3F 12510 seen at Moor Row in August 1947. P HUGHES

Even more minor souls such as J71 8286, another York engine, were treated to Apple green, in this case set off by a polished brass safety valve cover August 1947. P HUGHES

Representing the LNER in black is 7659, an O6, although much more readily recognised as a Stanier 8F which was caught on film at March in October 1945. Many engines that received wartime black were only lettered NE rather than LNER, and that applied even to A4 Pacifics. P HUGHES

LOCOMOTIVE LIVERIES IN 1948
EX GREAT WESTERN RAILWAY ENGINES

The Nationalisation period opened on January 1, 1948 with the only instructions to the regions being to apply a letter prefix to the existing running number and put the words 'British Railways' on the tender or tank side. The Western Region had the least to do to conform to any new requirements that British Railways might impose in as much as, believed to be due to its cast cabside number plates, it was allowed to retain its existing locomotive numbers when a new numbering scheme was advised later in the year, so the only change was the brief use of the 'W' prefix' to denote ownership. As time moved on even its livery colours remained almost unchanged for many classes. ■

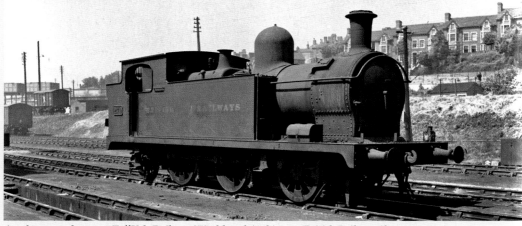

Another example was ex Taff Vale Railway 270 although in this case 'British Railways' has been applied in Great Western style lettering and a front number plate has yet to be fitted.

A close up of the number plate of Ex Barry Railway tank 263 shows the GWR lettering that was used on most absorbed engine plates. Above is the route disc and power classification letter whilst below is the 'W' applied as part of the initial renumbering scheme. This picture dates from 1951. T OWEN

A place one might have expected the corporate paint brush to miss was the Llanfair narrow gauge system but resident 823 has clearly received a W to go with its number even if there is no other evidence of either GW or BR ownership as late as June 1954. J McCANN

ABOVE: *County class 1002 **County of Berks** appears to be almost ex-works although it has reached its home shed of Bristol Bath Road as evidenced by the 'BRD' painted on the cylinder cover. All-over black has been applied as has a minimal amount of cream lining whilst the tender awaits the application of the lion and wheel emblem in April 1949.* W BOYDEN

A disproportionate number of the ex-constituent company tanks from South Wales seem to have been painted with British Railways on the tank sides with ex Rhymney Railway 73 being a typical example. However, note the minutiae of painting on the number plate where the G and R have been painted over leaving just the W visible.

Another Welsh descendent was Alexandra Dock Railway 0-6-0T 666 seen at Newport Pill in June 1949. Again, it carries British Railways in GW style but unlike the previous two examples it correctly carries its route disc and power classification above the number plate.

The date is August 1959 but 2251 class 2286 still displays British Railways in GW style on its tender, this being applied to all-over black paint. Only the Yellow route disc and red buffer beam enliven the scene. Remarkably unlined black 3208 lasted without any tender crest into the 1960s and even acquired electrification flashes in that state.

LEFT: *Thought to be the only Dean Goods to receive lined black livery is 2579 seen here at Didcot in April 1950. Although devoid of any tender markings the lining can be seen on the splashers and boiler. The 'DID' shed code is painted just behind the buffer beam but would shortly be replaced by a shed plate. The engine received the lining at the time it was selected for comparison trials with the then quite new Ivatt Class 2 2-6-0s.* S TOWNROE

BELOW LEFT: *Early lining on black locomotives took in only the cab and tender and here we have yet another GW loco without its lion and wheel totem despite the date being at some time post January 1950 as the engine, 5967 Bickmarsh Hall, is fitted with its Banbury shed plate.*

MAIN PICTURE: *Both Castle 4037* The South Wales Borderers *and 0-6-0PT 3694 are seen at Shrewsbury in April 1949 with British Railways in GW style applied. A close study of 3694 shows that the 'W' has been applied below the number plate.*

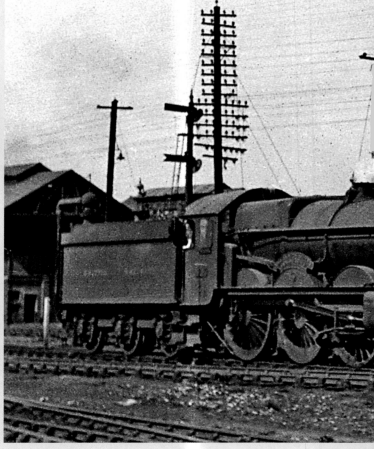

Whilst the Dean Goods should probably not have received any lining, the Saints certainly should and 2947 Madresfield Court *displays its livery at Reading in June 1950 but again, without any evidence of ownership. Some members of the class had red backed name and number plates. The route disc is prominent on the cabside.* P HUGHES

An unusual, for the time, panned shot of 2-8-0 4700 shows it to be bereft of all markings save its route disc which is just visible on the cabside - a vision in black at Chippenham in 1949. **K Leach**

ABOVE: 6658 looks clean considering that its black paintwork might have been applied prior to 1948 but the lettering style would certainly mean it had not been renewed since early 1949. This picture is dated August 8, 1954, taken at Barry where the cleaners have ensured that the safety valve cover and copper capped chimney have received the treatment. Safety valve covers were often painted over on freight classes. R BROUGHTON

LEFT: The claimed date for this picture of May 1948 is problematical as the engine 6987 *Shervington Hall* looks to be ex-works. However, it was new in March 1948 so unless it was quickly returned to the works the latter date would seem more likely. Note the lining which has not been applied to the cylinders but does go up and over the cab window. The buffer beam number does not repeat the 'W' branding applied to the cabside. A C STERNDALE

For a couple of years Granges and Manors ran in unlined black as seen here on Manor 7802 **Bradley Manor** at Llanbadarn on May 11, 1951. Most graduated to lined black, quite often with red backed plates and later to lined green after 1956. Various coaching stock liveries complete the picture. T OWEN

EX SOUTHERN RAILWAY ENGINES

In the main, engines inherited from the Southern Railway carried Malachite green for the passenger classes and unlined black for the rest but with many carrying their numbers and other markings in the so-called 'sunshine style'. They were renumbered by the addition of 30,000 to their numbers except for those using the notation introduced by Oliver Bulleid with the Q1s becoming 33001-40, the West Country / Battle of Britain group 34XXX series numbers with the Merchant Navies becoming 35001-30. Some other minor number changes also took place. ■

LEFT: *For a brief period Southern engines that used the numbering system introduced by Bulleid ran with those numbers before being changed to the 3XXXX series and some acquired the 's' prefix- the Southern always applied this in front of the number unlike the Western who put it beneath. 21C107 Wadebridge became 34007. Note that the tender carries British Railways, all applied on Malachite green in 'Sunshine' style.* J SUTTON

RIGHT: *The Southern Railway had many medium sized tanks of which the M7s were one. 30039 displays the standard black paint scheme but the lining appears to be simply a single cream band. The shed plate would suggest that the engine is at Exmouth Junction, but it looks more like Plymouth Friary where it was reallocated in March 1951. Note that the bunker lining goes up as high as possible and lines up with that on the tank side, although the latter is not placed equally between the top and bottom of the tank.*

The USA tanks were traditionally painted black although late in life a few were painted in Malachite green as we shall see. Here, what was Southern Railway 73 has become Southern Region s73 seen at Southampton Docks in 1949.

ABOVE: *Although one of few ex LSWR 0-6-0s, the black livery applied to 0395 class 30571 was typical of the fleet and is seen here at Eastleigh in 1950. It had carried 3154 as a Southern Railway engine.*

LEFT: *We have two pictures of King Arthurs in Malachite green. Here we see s787 Sir Menaduke with all lettering/numbers in Sunshine style. Note that the Southern applied the 's' effectively in lower case, being smaller than the number and that the number also appeared on the back of the tender. This picture dates from 1948.* **S TOWNROE**

Whilst many Southern 4-4-0s eventually carried lined black this was not the case for L12 30425 which is in standard unlined black. No power classification was carried at this time. The engine was withdrawn in mid-1951.

The British Railways Steam Years From 1948

RIGHT: *An early colour view shows 0415 30582 in its full lined black glory save the lack of any branding or totem. Note that the power classification has been applied. Eastleigh, October 1949. S TOWNROE*

BELOW: *Clearly C14 0-4-0T 30589 could not carry its number on its bunker or cabside so the only option was to place it centrally below the British Railways branding which itself was in a smaller size than usual. Note the Sunshine style number of 30109 alongside. Eastleigh 1949.*

BELOW RIGHT: *In May 1949 30774 Sir Gaheris now has BR style numbers and awaits its lion and wheel emblem. The colour of older transparencies is always difficult to get right, but it is clear that whilst the locomotive has the contemporary style numbers etc. the paint scheme is still SR Malachite.*

Under the BR livery scheme lined black appeared on a number of classes that had previously been plain black. Us and Ns such as 31850 received lining although, at least on this example, not on the boiler or cylinders. Note how the tender lining briefly follows the tender outline at the top corners. Stewarts Lane, September 16, 1950. Unlike the other companies, Southern engines bore no outward sign of depot allocation until shed plates were introduced from 1950. G H Hunt

BELOW: E5 0-6-2T 32406 has just cream lining on its black paintwork and the lion and wheel are absent some two years after their introduction. Compare the lining with that on M7 30039. On the E5 it sweeps up to the top of the bunker but the top of the tank lining level matches that on the bunker before the upsweep. There is no attempt to line the front portion of the E5's cabside. W BOYDEN

L Class 31762 displays variations compared to 31166 below whereby the lining is not continuous on the splashers and there is no sign of ownership when ex-works at Ashford on July 16, 1949. J SUTTON

RIGHT: *E4 tank s2497, later 32497 appears to have just had a quick visit to the repair shops as its smokebox has been repainted but clearly shows how the 'S' prefix was applied. However, the rest of its black paint looks like it is long overdue for replacement.*

BELOW RIGHT: *The E1 tanks were one of three classes of locomotive to work on the Isle of Wight, this one carrying unlined black livery. The numbers carried by engines on the island duplicated those in use on the mainland. The IOW engines were not included in the Southern 3XXXX renumbering scheme but confusingly were designated to carry a number with a W prefix. Photographic evidence suggests however that the 'W' only ever appeared on a small oval plate carried on the back of the bunker. Isle of Wight engines did not carry smokebox number plates. 3 Ryde is seen in September 1951. M J READE*

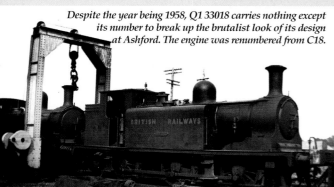

Despite the year being 1958, Q1 33018 carries nothing except its number to break up the brutalist look of its design at Ashford. The engine was renumbered from C18.

We are now nearly seven years after nationalisation on 12th September 1954 but E class 31166 still carries the British Railways lettering but without its front number plate. Compare this with that carried by D class 31737 behind, which has acquired the lion and wheel emblem and running plate lining. T OWEN

EX LONDON MIDLAND & SCOTTISH RAILWAY ENGINES

In the main, former LMS locomotives were in some form of black livery at the 1st January 1948 and had 40000 added to their previous number, once carrying an M prefix to the pre 1948 number was discontinued. However, limited complete renumbering took place on some pre-grouping locomotives to bring them within the 40000-58999 range. ■

RIGHT: Former LMS compound 40929 is resplendent in full BR lined black livery, although not graced with lining on either boiler or cylinder. On the tender, lining only follows the bottom 'panel' rather than the outline of the tender. An unexplained 'mystery disc' appears to be painted above the power classification on the cabside. P HUGHES

Despite its higher running number, 42199 was built at Derby works and delivered five months earlier than 42165 seen later, which was also constructed there, but having a different paint scheme of unlined black with large numbers. It and fellow classmate 42198 were rapidly despatched to the Southern Region after building for evaluation which resulted in a number of members of the class being allocated to the Southern for passenger duties.

Crab 42783 displays the full lining treatment combined with the British Railways branding. The boiler and cylinders are lined in red, the rest of the lining being the cream and red combination. **P HUGHES**

Although undated, this picture of Ivatt 2MT 41219 was almost certainly taken in September 1948 when the locomotive was new and thus it never carried LMS livery, only the first ten of the class being built by the LMS. Whilst there appeared to be room to put the number on the bunker side the decision was taken to put it on the cabside and thus there was no lining on the bunker. The figures on the number plate are in a non-standard font. **P HUGHES**

1F M1708 will have been renumbered thus in the first three or so months of 1948 but by July 10, 1949 had not been dealt with further to comply with the BR standard livery. In fact, it is a hybrid as whilst it carries M1708 on the bunker it has not been given an M prefix to its LMS style front number plate.

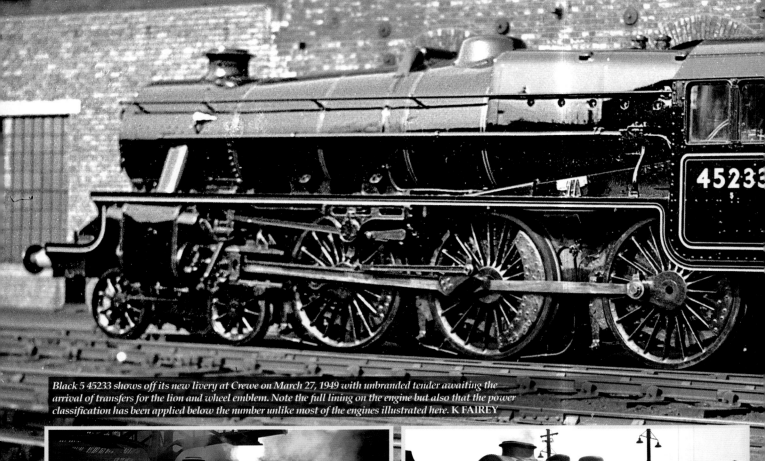

Black 5 45233 shows off its new livery at Crewe on March 27, 1949 with unbranded tender awaiting the arrival of transfers for the lion and wheel emblem. Note the full lining on the engine but also that the power classification has been applied below the number unlike most of the engines illustrated here. K FAIREY

42165 appears to carry the livery in which it was new in August 1948 although we are seeing it on June 1, 1950. Clearly much loved by a crew at Hamilton shed, it has also been adorned with extensive white paint at the front end.

Like the Ivatt and Fairburn tanks already seen, Ivatt 4MT 43007 was delivered new to British Railways, in this case on 1 February 1948. However, this predated the decision on a new numbering system and thus the engine emerged as M3007 and is seen here in May 1949 at Carnforth. The engine would later be rebuilt with a single chimney. W BOYDEN

Jubilee 45588 Kashmir carries LMS lined black but devoid of any evidence of ownership. However, both the cabside and smokebox numbers have been applied in corporate style although possibly the cabside numbers are white rather than cream. The power classification is below the number. Polmadie 1949. J ROBERTSON

Plain black always adorned the vast number of LMS 0-6-0s and so there is little to complicate this view of M4236 (later 44236) save to note that it does not carry an 'M' on the smokebox and the font of the smokebox numbers differs from that used on M3007 in the previous view. This image was taken at Millhouses shed. P HUGHES

Wartime austerity had seen many Stanier Black 5s turned out in unlined black, a state that persisted at nationalisation. 5018 became M5018 before later becoming 45018. Note the number extremely high on the cabside and the front number plate with the later LMS font but no 'M' prefix.

Princess 46212 Duchess of Kent appears to be carrying BR lined black in this view taken at Shrewsbury.

LEFT: *Ex LNWR 1P 2-4-2T 46656 was unique in its class in being allocated to a Scottish Region shed and at this time it was Beattock, dating the picture as post June 1949. No front number is carried and was one probably never fitted as very few Webb designed engines ever carried one. No power classification can be seen either.*

RIGHT: *Five years after the formation of British Railways and four since its new crest was introduced, ex-Caledonian 0-4-4T is living very much in the past at Forfar on July 18, 1953. The all-over black livery still looks smart and is corporately correct unlike the locomotive behind which has the large 10" numbers often found on Scottish engines.*

BELOW: *A rare image in colour of ex-Lancashire and Yorkshire Railways 4-6-0 50455 helps us to see that it is in full lined black livery. The picture was taken at York in July 1951, apparently on its final working.*

Clearly freshly painted and just ex works at Horwich is ex-Lancashire and Yorkshire 0-6-0ST M11375 in plain black. However, it appears not to have had its front number plate fitted but will eventually become 51375. Note the position of the 2F power classification.

52465 was one of a few ex-Lancashire & Yorkshire 0-6-0s to stray well off home territory to find a new home at Nuneaton where it is seen in November 1950. All appears to be in order with its unlined black livery except the non-application of its power classification.

Despite having a 4P power classification, the small class of ex-Caledonian 4-6-2 tanks seem to have only been worthy of unlined black livery. That is certainly the case for 55352 seen here and which has yet to be given its lion and wheel emblem despite the date being June 2, 1950. T OWEN.

Already past its 60th birthday, ex LMS 1F 58040 carries fully compliant unlined black save for the lack of its power classification. This engine was renumbered directly from 1273. The 20C shed plate dates the view to between August 1952 and October 1954.

Possibly following the LMS paint scheme, the ex-North London 0-6-0 tanks initially had their new identities applied with the number underneath the British Railways lettering rather than on the cabside. Clearly symmetry was the order of the day with the M number prefix being placed centrally above the number. M27510 became 58852 under the new numbering scheme.

58040 was a youngster compared to Midland 2F 0-6-0 58110, the design dating from 1868 and it survived until 1951. Unusually the locomotive appears to have a crudely painted front number to complement its unlined black livery.

EX LONDON & NORTH EASTERN RAILWAY ENGINES

All Former LNER locomotives were to be renumbered with the addition of 60,000 to their numbers. Under the post war LNER management most A4 Pacifics had reverted to Garter blue whilst many other classes were receiving Apple green to replace the wartime austerity black, with only pure freight engines supposed to be repainted black. ■

RIGHT: *To the trained eye, despite this being a black and white view of A4 60008* **Dwight D Eisenhower** *at Heaton shed on July 8, 1949 LNER Garter blue is evident. Note the class designation and allocation between the buffers, BR shed codes were not introduced until 1950.* **T OWEN**

LEFT: *A2/3 60517* **Ocean Swell** *has had its new number and branding applied to LNER Apple green in standard fashion which did not include any lining on the cabside. It is unclear if the front number plate is fitted. The picture dates from 1949.* **E SANDERSON**

BELOW: *The full application of the BR standard requirements is evident here with an August 1949 view of B17/4 61668* **Bradford City** *at Marks Tey. The buffer beam carries the loco allocation and is lined in white.* **G W POWELL**

K3/2 61945 displays standard lined black at Doncaster which includes the boiler bands, cylinders and running board. The allocation however remains on the buffer beam as no shed plate is carried. Note the carriage in the background still in LNER teak livery. P HUGHES

BELOW LEFT: *The two V4 2-6-2s were quite camera shy but 61700 Bantam Cock is shown here apparently carrying BR lined black although it is unclear if it is just cream lining or with the additional thin red line. The picture has been taken in 1950 or later as the engine carries the 65A Eastfield shed plate.*

BELOW: *North of the border we see D41 62246 at Keith in May 1950. Note the splasher and boiler lining although there does not appear to be any below the running plate. The shed allocation appears on the buffer beam despite a shed plate being fitted. The LNER route availability (RA) is under the number inside the cab lining. T OWEN*

The Q4 0-8-0s were an early casualty of BR withdrawals with the last being condemned in 1951. Here 63225 carries the British Railways branding, front number plate and shed plate on plain black. Due to the early demise of the class it is possible that none carried the lion and wheel emblem. P HUGHES

BR lined black is also carried by K2/2 61756, again at Eastfield in 1951. Note that despite being replaced by the lion and wheel in 1949, British Railways lettering remained to be seen for a number of years. Note how the cabside numbers have had to be compressed in order to get them within the lining. W BOYDEN

A rare view of D10 62658 **Prince George** at an exhibition at Chesterfield Market Place in August 1948 to mark the centenary of the death of George Stephenson. Note that the lining is only in cream and the route availability is outside the cab lining. This is thought to be the only member of the class to have been lined in combination with the British Railways lettering. P HUGHES

The British Railways Steam Years From 1948

Details of where the bulk of locomotive re-numberings took place are lost in the mists of time, but many must have been done at the locomotive's home shed. The appearance of J39/2 64872 suggests that the minimum amount of cleaning and preparation took place to apply the number and branding. The engine is at Dukinfield wagon works. No sign of the 'RA' markings but perhaps they are under the grime. P HUGHES

A rare colour view depicts J36 65330 carrying its BR trappings on LNER Apple green livery. However, it has not acquired a front number plate and the RA designation is just to the bottom right of the cabside number. Dundee 1949. J ROBERTSON

ABOVE: In a typically begrimed state, J11 64422 carries plain black livery but large cabside numbers on July 10, 1949 at Staveley shed. The application of shed plates is still six months away. P HUGHES

LEFT: An early adopter of the correct British Railways livery (8" cabside numbers had still not been specified) was O1 63773 as it was chosen to take part in the 1948 exchange trials and is seen here at Acton Yard.

MAIN PICTURE: C13 67409 was typical of the LNER 4-4-2Ts in terms of livery application with lining on the tank and bunker sides with the number on the bunker. In this case the British Railways branding is larger than standard with the 'RA' designation carried at the bottom left of the tank lining. There appears to be lining on the side of the running plate. P HUGHES

Only 20 J5 0-6-0s were built and all were condemned by 1955 with most eking out an existence at Colwick shed. Here 65496 displays plain black with the RA markings at the bottom right of the cabside and no shed plate. P HUGHES

ABOVE: The classes of smaller tanks presented problems for the painters in that on occasions there was insufficient space to apply the livery as per the specification, leading to variations from engine to engine depending on where the application took place. However, in the case of Y9 68104 all appears well although the 'RA' designation is placed centrally on the cabside. Polmont, August 17, 1953. E Bruton

LEFT: N4/4 69244 shows off an interesting set of variations with both the lettering and number being too large (compare to the tank engine behind) and it also does not appear to be carrying an 'RA' designation. At withdrawal the whole class was allocated to Sheffield Darnall where this picture was taken on March 26, 1950. T OWEN

On the Z Class tanks it was decided that there was insufficient room for the number to go on the bunker, so it was placed centrally on the tank side beneath the British Railways branding. However, in this case on 68192, the branding is in a non-standard size. Kittybrewster, May 29, 1950. T OWEN

On a J83 tank there was just room to put the number on the side of the bunker. A shed plate has yet to arrive in the case of 68446. At least one member of this class carried BR markings on Apple green. W BOYDEN

ABOVE: An uncomplicated side on most Sentinel locomotives allowed the painters to do their work. That work had apparently only just been completed at the time that this picture of Y1/2 68159 was taken, as painting marker lines can be seen both for the RA and Class designations. Note that as far as is known, Sentinel locomotives never carried front number plates. This one has the 'No' painted ahead of its buffer beam applied number. T Owen

LEFT: One locomotive guaranteed to cause a challenge to any corporate painting scheme was Garratt 69999. Here the British Railways branding has been applied below the boiler and the number applied to just one of the water tanks. Bromsgrove 1949.

WAR DEPARTMENT LOCOMOTIVES

The War Department tender locomotives have been included with details of the BR Standard types for ease of reference although the first of those to enter traffic did not do so until 1951. WD locomotives had a unique position at Nationalisation as some 200 were in LNER stock having been their class O7 whilst the rest were still viewed as 'on loan' to the various companies. However, all that were either inherited from the LNER or purchased by BR were then allocated 9XXXX series numbers under the new BR numbering system. ∎

BELOW RIGHT: *Scottish Region allocated WD 2-10-0 90774 shows how all the WDs should have looked from spring 1948 with British Railways on the tender and a smokebox number plate.*

BELOW: *The allocated livery for WDs was plain black. No date was recorded for this picture, but the unmarked tender would suggest mid 1949 when the decision was taken to replace 'British Railways' lettering with the lion and wheel emblem but the transfers were not yet available. However, note the buffer beam number 90719, which suggests a much earlier view. The cabside numbers are also non-standard appearing to be 10" rather than 8" high. The engine had been WD 79271 and was allocated to Gloucester although the picture appears to be taken at Doncaster.* P HUGHES

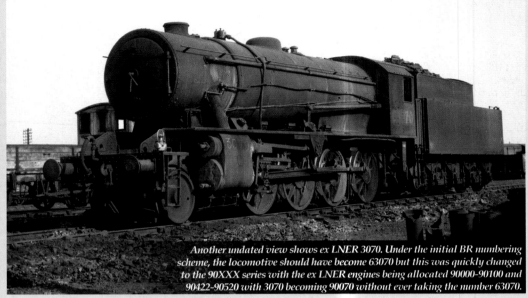

Another undated view shows ex LNER 3070. Under the initial BR numbering scheme, the locomotive should have become 63070 but this was quickly changed to the 90XXX series with the ex LNER engines being allocated 90000-90100 and 90422-90520 with 3070 becoming 90070 without ever taking the number 63070.

LIVERY VARIATIONS OF EARLY NATIONALISATION
EX GREAT WESTERN RAILWAY LOCOMOTIVES

In the previous section the pictures illustrated how British Railways intended that its locomotive fleet should look until experiments had taken place to decide on a livery policy for the years to come. Even within those pictures there are minor variances from the plan.

Now we explore in more detail the vast array of combinations of lettering, numbering and painting differences that were the practical result of renumbering, starting with the Western Region. ■

Ex Taff Vale Railway 0-6-2T 204 is seen at Aberdare on June 17, 1951. Despite being well over three years since Nationalisation it proudly displays GWR on its tank sides but in a font that is much like that required by BR rather than anything applied by the Great Western. It does however have its smokebox number plate and shed plate although still carrying its painted GW allocation lettering as well. T OWEN

Another view from 1951, is this time at Ferndale with Taff Vale 0-6-2T 279 carrying British Railways in Great Western Style. It too has its shed plate but does not carry a smokebox number plate. T OWEN

1366 class 0-6-0T 1370 appears not to have received a major overhaul in at least seven years as on April 17, 1955 it still has GWR lettering on its tank side. As would be expected by this date it does however carry its shed and front number plates. R BROUGHTON

2021 Class pannier tank 2131 still carries 'GWR' on the tank side but has both front number and shed plates putting the date of the view as 1950 or later.

Given that the tender of Star 4059 **Princess Patricia** *retains its Great Western branding, this locomotive is most likely to be in GW green livery with the only nod to its BR ownership being the front number plate and shed plate. The view, taken at Iver, dates from October 5, 1950.* G H HUNT

Despite the grime, the livery details of 1901 Class pannier 1968 can be seen, these being British Railways in Great Western style lettering. Note the number on the front buffer beam and the shed code below the running plate at the front. Birkenhead May 29, 1949. T OWEN

5101 class 2-6-2T 4129 still carries wartime austerity black complete with GWR lettering at Parkgate in August 1954. Under the initial BR scheme, the plain black is correct at this time, but not of course the GWR branding. The '6C' shed plate, for Birkenhead, shows that day to day operation of the engine was the responsibility of the Midland Region. J MCCANN

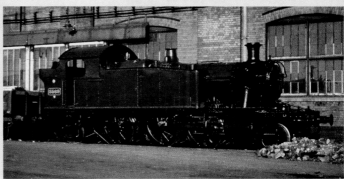

ABOVE: Illustrating that nothing is predictable with railway liveries is this view of apparently ex-works 4575 class tank 5569, which is dated May 1948. By this time the use of the 'w' notation should have ceased but the letter is obviously carried, and the tank side should carry 'British Railways' but is clearly unadorned. Similarly, no front number plate has been fitted. A C STERNDALE

LEFT: Another illustration of how the Great Western lived on in the BR era. Here we have 5800 Class 0-4-2T 5801 still carrying GWR on the tanks, apparently on a black base in July 1958. The engine was condemned two months later and so almost certainly never carried any of the three versions of BR livery that could have been applied by then. The class, along with the similar 14XX carried neither route disc or power letter as they were 'unclassified' in both systems. P H WELLS

ABOVE: *One of the challenges to applying the right livery to a model is that of tender swaps, a practise that became increasingly common as the end of steam loomed. Here we see 5980 Dingley Hall correctly carrying lined black livery but being paired with a green tender carrying GW branding.*

RIGHT: *Wales harboured an unusually large number of engines that did not gain BR identity in a hurry. 74XX 7417 continues to show its GW ancestry on black in May 1951 and the Dukedog behind has yet to get a front number plate despite the late date. T Owen*

BELOW: *The date is August 27, 1961 and yet here we find 9710, one of the condensing pannier tanks, still carrying the GWR shirt button emblem at Old Oak Common. As the application of this style ceased in mid-1942 at best, the engine had worked for 19 years without a repaint and possibly longer. T OWEN*

EX SOUTHERN RAILWAY LOCOMOTIVES

Unlike the Western Region the Southern had to renumber its locomotives and in due course replace its Malachite green with the shade chosen by British Railways, but Malachite continued to be applied into 1949 giving rise to plenty of non-standard liveries appearing. ■

ABOVE RIGHT: *T9 30119 was at one time designated as a Royal engine by the Southern. As such it was kept in immaculate condition. Although not completely clear, it seems to have the cabside number applied in Gill Sans font on lined Malachite green whilst the tender lettering is clearly in Sunshine style as is the retained number on the back of the tender. It is seen at Waterloo on May 23, 1950.* **T OWEN**

RIGHT: *Showing the need for creativity, some classes, such as the 0415 tanks, had insufficient space to display the required numbers and words at standard size. The need to squeeze British Railways onto the tank sides has led to the decision to apply the number at reduced size to match. As 30584 is in Eastleigh works it will almost certainly have emerged carrying full size numbers along with the lion and wheel emblem. June 2, 1951.* **T OWEN**

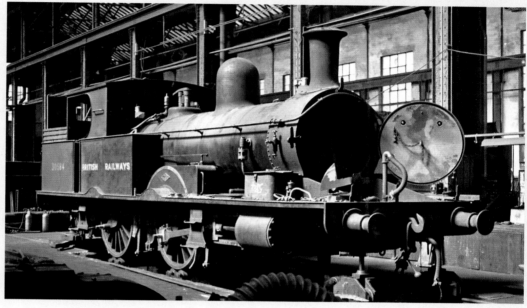

Malachite green was used extensively and was even deemed appropriate for an M7 tank, as seen here on 30038 at Nine Elms in March 1950. Traces of green can be seen on the wheels, but Sunshine lettering has been superseded by the standard Gill Sans font. A front number plate has been fitted but the shed plate has yet to appear.

*The first of two examples of the application of details in Gill Sans font on Malachite green shows Lord Nelson 30862 **Lord Collingwood** at Bournemouth on a Winter Gardens Society special.* **R BROUGHTON**

*Secondly we see Schools class 30928 **Stowe** at Newhaven in April 1949. There is black edging to the number but not to the tender lettering. No power classification or any other symbol appeared on the cabsides at this time.* **F HORNBY**

The initial application of its new number and lettering on R1 0-6-0T 31154 followed the layout used by the Southern Railway. All, including the buffer beam number, have been applied in 'Sunshine' style.

D Class 4-4-0 31733 had just 12 months left in service when photographed at Brighton in 1952. Carrying overall black, note the number 1733 below the running plate behind the buffer beam. Sunshine style cabside number and a tender on which both of its recent owner's names can be discerned complete the scene.

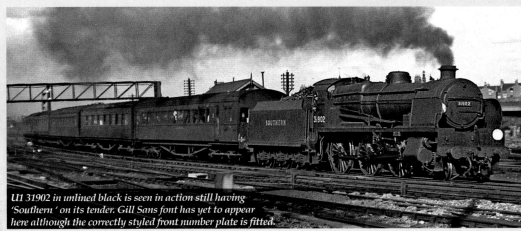

U1 31902 in unlined black is seen in action still having 'Southern' on its tender. Gill Sans font has yet to appear here although the correctly styled front number plate is fitted.

Given that engines such as U class 31622 were more frontline power than some on the Southern it might have been expected that by June 1951 they would have acquired the full corporate livery. However, the only nod to BR here is the application of the revised cabside number.

ABOVE: *The IIX class consisted of ten engines with the majority being condemned in 1948. 32005, seen here at Eastbourne, was the last of class, being withdrawn in June 1951. The picture illustrates that initially the Southern Region continued to apply a number to the bunker (or tender) on some engines. In this case there is a space in the middle of the number on the back of the bunker whilst those on the side are applied in a smaller size than usual.* W Boyden

LEFT: *The O2 tanks based on the Isle of Wight were used for the majority of the passenger duties and the Southern Region clearly thought that this should be recognised by the use of fully lined Malachite green. The number is carried on the buffer beam, another anomaly that persisted throughout the life of steam on the island. 32 Bonchurch is seen at Freshwater on May 18, 1952.* T OWEN

A total one-off livery combination was that which appeared on West Country 34006 Bude which was selected to take part in the 1948 exchange trails. It is seen here at Aylesbury in June of that year. As such it had to conform to the BR standard as much as possible, so it has its new number in Gill Sans font but has not been fitted with a number plate. The 'Southern' smokebox door ring remains in place. Because the Southern engines were not fitted with scoops to take water from troughs, for duties away from the region it was paired with a Stanier tender painted unlined black with 'British Railways' in white, also in Gill Sans font.

EX LONDON MIDLAND & SCOTTISH RAILWAY LOCOMOTIVES

O
n the Midland Region most locomotives were painted black although a handful of red ones remained. However, two different fonts had been in use recently which led to an interesting mixture of variants when renumbering took place.

RIGHT: *The LMS Compounds had been one of the classes to run in red livery but it would seem that 41171 has long since lost that in favour of wartime black. Seen here in June 1951, at its home shed of Dumfries, it has the correctly applied 'British Railways' but the running number is larger than standard and whilst it has lost its LMS front number plate it has not received the BR version. It was withdrawn at the end of 1952.* K FAIREY

LEFT: *Here we see a typical Midland renumbering leaving LMS intact on the tank sides and putting on the new number in the matching, but already superseded, font. This view of 3P 40070, formerly LMS 70 was taken at Tebay.*

BELOW: *Unlined black again featured on Stanier 3P 40190 but here we see that the number has been replaced in the designated Gill Sans style whilst LMS has been retained. Whilst the smokebox number plate is just visible it is not possible to see if that had been changed. The LMS had been the only company to fit smokebox number plates.*

LEFT: *Former London, Tilbury and Southend 3P 41960 had been renumbered from 2142 using extra-large Gill Sans numbers on unlined black whilst retaining LMS on the tanks. No front number plate was carried at this time, July 21, 1948. H C Casserley*

RIGHT: *Stanier 5MT 45096 had been renumbered with commendable speed by its Scottish owners. Its home shed of Kingmoor was deemed to be part of that region in May 1948 although it is seen here at Polmadie. The cabside numbers are large and do not appear to be of quite the right style whilst the original front number plate has been removed but not yet replaced. K FAIREY*

Jubilee 45696 **Arethusa** *has been renumbered in a similar style to Black 5 45096, but the numbers have been placed closer to the cab windows. The locomotive at least carries some form of lining, this probably being in the LNWR style on black. The Fowler tender is too grimy to discern if it too is lined but the LMS lettering is in block style. A BR style number plate adorns the smokebox door.*

Royal Scot 46110 **Grenadier Guardsman** *appears to have just received some minor maintenance at Crewe Works on March 27, 1949, possibly including its renumbering. The locomotive carries LNW style lined black with block LMS lettering and the new-style front number plate. However, unlike the Black 5 and Jubilee seen previously it has its power classification below the cabside number.* **K FAIREY**

Ivatt 2MT 46406 is again in unlined black. The locomotive is correct in its BR attire, but the tender retains LMS lettering. Leeds City June 25, 1949. **G H HUNT**

Another visitor to Crewe Works has been dealt with in much the same style. In addition, Princess Coronation 46253 **City of St Albans** *has had part of its lining repainted but there is no sign of either its former or new smokebox number plate.*

Extra-large numbers again feature on 7F 49230 although what, if anything, lies beneath the grime on the tender we shall never know. This picture was taken at Warrington on May 26, 1950. T OWEN

Large cabside numbers would not have been an option on Pug 51232 although the tank side is sufficient for a normal size of LMS lettering. A BR style number plate has been fitted. J SUTTON

LEFT: *As one of the Crewe Works shunters, the Bissel tank, 47865, should perhaps have been one of the first engines to receive the full and correct BR treatment. However, its lowly duties might have determined otherwise. On March 27, 1949 it has large cabside numbers but no front number plate. Two further examples of renumbering variety lurk in the background with 58XXX 0-6-0s displaying vastly different sized cabside numbers.*

As in other regions, the smaller tank classes could pose a challenge to the painters but in this variant of the 47XXX 0-4-0STs the tank and cabside are of sufficient size to carry the BR number 47004 in LMS style but with LMS lettering.

Clan 4-6-0 54767 Clan Mackinnon was the sole survivor of its class to be taken into BR stock. Due to the position of the tablet catcher the BR number, in large numerals, has been placed high on the cabside. The number plate is hard to read but appears to be in the BR style.

Staying in Scotland we find former Caledonian 0-6-0 57323, again in plain black, simply adorned with an oversize cabside number and the correctly sized British Railways on the tender. The power classification is well up on the cabside as it was in the view of 54767. Note the shed plate, mounted high up on the smokebox door, where the non-existent number plate should be.

1P 0-4-4T 58076 was previously LMS number 1396. The renumbering has been done to match the style of the LMS on the tank side. However, the locomotive is clean enough to see that the tank side lettering is shaded in black which appears not to be the case with the numbers. P HUGHES

RIGHT: *Big Bertha, 58100, could have been a one-off in style when it came to application of the BR identity. However, in this view, along with the persistent LMS tender lettering, the cabside number is in the matching style although smaller than usual whilst the smokebox number plate is pure BR.*

BELOW: *We previously saw M27510 (page 26) from this class with a completely different layout of number and ownership information. 58859, previously 27522 is not following any BR convention as in theory the number should have been applied on the cabside but that would have left 'LMS' isolated at the end of the side tank. The disparity in sizes does not help the appearance. The final BR version saw the BR totem placed centrally on the tank with the number beneath it. The locomotive is pictured at Devons Road, April 24, 1949. K FAIREY*

EX LONDON & NORTH EASTERN RAILWAY LOCOMOTIVES

The Eastern Region had put engines from a number of classes into Apple green by the start of 1948 and so variations could occur, both with the green - which continued to be applied to express engines for some time - and unlined black. Initially all LNER stock had 60,000 added to the number until the Class O7 WDs went into the 90XXX series. ∎

RIGHT: *With a number of E1391, at first glance it might be assumed that we are looking at a B1 but this is a member of the B7/1 class. It was renumbered, at least on paper, to 61711 and withdrawn in July 1950, over a year before B1 61391 was built. The E has been applied in the same style and position as used on the Southern Region. In theory this engine was the subject of two visits to the painters as the 'E' had been superseded by the use of a '6' by the time the British Railways legend was applied.* P HUGHES

BELOW: *The B1s were another class that enjoyed the use of Apple green as seen here on 61163 but again with large sized cabside numbers and no front number plate. The loco is seen here double heading with black painted 61126 at Amersham on September 20, 1948.* G H HUNT

Displaying its Apple green livery to good effect A2/2 60504 Mons Meg is seen at Darlington. However, the cabside numbers are over size and there is no front number plate.

Another class to receive Apple green was some of the B12s, especially those north of the border, where we find B12/4 61508 at Kittybrewster in September 1949. Being apparently ex-works, the white lining on the wheels is clearly evident.

Another E prefixed engine was J11/3 4404 still running as such at Mexborough on March 26, 1950. T OWEN

RIGHT: *J24 65609 was a further engine displaying just NE on its tender with the cabside numbers being of intermediate size. The number is on the buffer beam where the shed allocation can just be discerned as can the route availability at the bottom left of the cab side sheet. Whitby July 8, 1949. T OWEN*

LEFT: *The LNER had taken wartime paint and labour saving to heart and ended up simply applying 'NE' to many of its engines as seen here on D33 62459 at Dunfermline in 1948. Large numbers have appeared on the cabside but there is no other evidence of a change to BR requirements.*

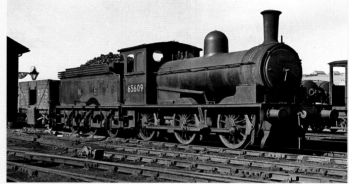

Like the B12 seen earlier, Apple green was applied enthusiastically in Scotland with another recipient being D11/2 62683 Hobbie Elliott seen in this image at Eastfield. Large numbers are again evident with a painted buffer beam number and depot allocation. 'RA' is painted low down at the corner of the cabside.

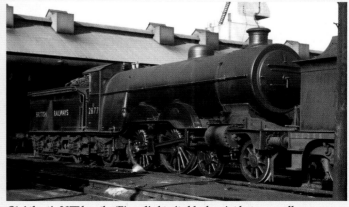

C1 Atlantic 2877 has the 'E' applied to its black paint but unusually it is above the number in this case. It is accompanied by cabside numbers and tender lettering in the correct size and style but no smokebox number plate has been applied. P HUGHES

Ex Darlington works in September 1948 is J26 65734. Unless work is not yet complete then it will have gone into traffic without its RA designation, painted allocation and any form of front number, although the bolts for the number plate are in place.

Looking for all the world as though the end is nigh is J25 E5696 with LNER on the tender. It was clearly revived later as it survived until 1958.

Moving on to the tank classes, here we have F5 67193 unusually displaying BR lined black. It was possibly afforded this honour as the class did primarily work passenger duties. With this paint job one would have expected a front number plate to have been fitted but the number is again on the buffer beam. The RA designation is below the 'B' of British Railways.

No mistaking the number of C13 tank 67477 although it might have been expected to be placed on the bunker side. Evidence of previous ownership is wearing away which is hardly surprising as it is now August 1953. E BRUTON

Plain and simple - a nice, prominent number and no evidence of any owner as found on Y9 68092 at Seafield on May 27, 1950. On this class the number was more typically put on the cabside than the tank. However, it does have its front number plate. T OWEN

L1 2-6-2T 67703 displays a similar number and name layout to that used on 67477 but this time it has been applied to Apple green paintwork. P HUGHES

ABOVE: *If ever there was a 'pet' engine it was Liverpool Street pilot E8619, later 68619, a J69. This engine was always kept immaculate and at this time carried Apple green livery.*

RIGHT: *Corporate paint schemes never seemed to fit the 'odds and ends' of a fleet. Here we see Sentinel Y3 class 8173 with its old number in shaded numerals with B.R. (E) applied in similar fashion. It is June 1952 at Lowestoft sleeper works and the Y3 has possibly been designated as a departmental locomotive which would account for the variance with policy. However, as we shall see later, most Eastern Region departmental locomotives clearly declared this in their paint scheme. T OWEN*

BELOW: *Some J72s were yet to be built but 68710 is one of the numerous original build seen at Kittybrewster on August 26, 1948. It's in unlined black with numbers that appear a little too large. No doubt a front number is carried under the grime on the front buffer beam but the 'RA' is just visible under the last 'S' of British Railways.*

THE EXPERIMENTAL LIVERIES OF 1948

Very soon after its formation, British Railways embarked upon a programme to evaluate new liveries for both its locomotives and rolling stock. Some of these are illustrated in the following pages. However, it must be appreciated that these are old colour images and the colour rendition may not be entirely accurate. ■

RIGHT: *Stanier 5MTs figured strongly in the locomotives chosen to display the new liveries. Black was not one of the featured liveries on a Stanier 5 but, according to various sources, a black member of the class just happened to pass by the place where various green painted class members were displayed and was thought to look better than those in the trial liveries. Subsequently 45292 was turned out as illustrated and shown to BR staff at Marylebone. Some 'plum and spilt milk' carriages can be seen in the background.*

RIGHT: *Three Stanier 5's were painted green carrying the numbers M4762 (Malachite), M4763 (Apple) and M4764 (Brunswick). The latter is seen in the Brunswick Green livery having been renumbered as 44764 along the way.*

BELOW: *Apple Green was chosen to be used on a number of engines. B17/6 61661 Sheffield Wednesday certainly looked smart when freshly painted and exhibited at Marylebone at the same time as 45292 above.*
A DOW COLLECTION

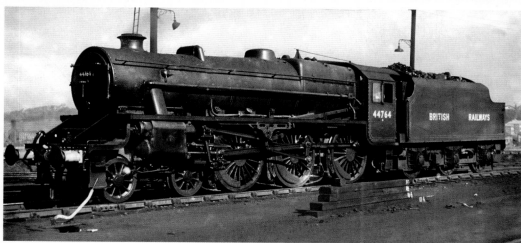

ABOCE: *A number of Castles were chosen to carry Apple green including some straight off the production line. An older class member, 4091 Dudley Castle, is seen at Chippenham with the light green treatment along with a non-standard front number plate. K Leach*

LEFT: *On the Midland it was the Patriots and Jubilees that gained Apple green. Jubilee 45565 Victoria was one example, note the red/orange lining. It is seen at Derby in 1948.*

BELOW: *The trial blue was a darker shade than that which was adopted later. Duchess 46241 City of Edinburgh shows this at Camden in April 1949. The lining was white and red.* W BOOT

RIGHT: *Not to be outdone, the Southern painted a Lord Nelson and a Bulleid Pacific in the new colour.* **30864 Sir Martin Frobisher** *is seen in close up at Southampton Docks in July 1948.* S TOWNROE

BELOW: *A startling apparition in a totally non-standard version of blue, and yet to be named* **East Asiatic Company,** *was Merchant Navy 35024. As can be seen, even the wheels were painted blue and the slab sides were broken up by the application of three bright red bands. The date is April 1949.* S TOWNROE

BELOW RIGHT: *A King carried the trial blue on the Western Region whilst on the Eastern, both A3 and A4 classes were used. A4 60028* **Walter K Wigham** *shows how the lining was applied below the running plate, a style that was not adopted for the selected lighter blue. It is seen at Grantham in June 1948.*

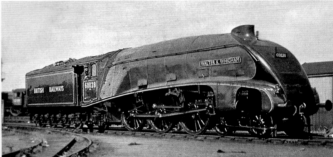

THE 1949 PAINTING SCHEME
EXPRESS PASSENGER BLUE

Following the evaluation of the livery trials carried out in 1948, three colours were decided upon for future use and they began to be applied in 1949. The most powerful express passenger engines were to be painted blue with black and white lining although the shade of blue was lighter than that used for the trials. However, such use did not last long as it was found that the paint faded and did not wear well, and the standard lined green replaced it from around 1953. All locomotives, regardless of the livery colour, would carry a new emblem of a wheel surmounted by a lion along with the with the words 'British Railways' passing through the centre of the wheel. This emblem could be applied in one of two sizes primarily dependent on the space available on the tank or tender side. Except on the Western Region, which retained its cast plates, Gill Sans numbers were to be applied to cabsides and these were specified as being 8in in height. Smoke box number plates were to use the same font although the numbers used on Western Region plates were an inch taller than those used elsewhere. ■

LEFT: *On the Western Region, only the Kings were selected to carry the blue livery. In July 1949 the region's star engine* 6000 King George V *was photographed at Chippenham in the new livery. The splashers and nameplate as well as the cylinders carry the lining.* K LEACH

BELOW: *Turning to the Midland Region, both Pacific classes qualified for an application of blue paint. Colour pictures of a Princess in blue are rare but here we see* 46206 Princess Marie Louise *at Rugby.*

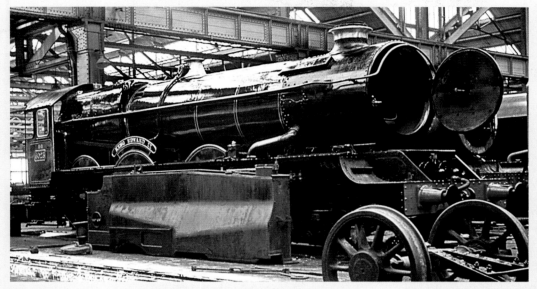

LEFT: *Blue was still being applied in March 1952 and this may well be at least the second time that 6023* King Edward II *had been so painted. It is seen in Swindon Works.* T OWEN

BELOW: *On the Southern Region only the Merchant Navy Pacifics qualified for blue livery and due to the air smoothed casing it was applied in a different style to that used elsewhere. The body style called for a black band flanked by two white lines running the full length of the engine and tender at the top and bottom. Areas beneath the bottom band were painted black. 35020* Bibby Line *also has a red backed nameplate. Places where the livery has been 'touched up' are clearly evident.* PURSEY C SHORT

With the additional fittings and decorations associated with the Golden Arrow, 35027 Port Line *stands at Victoria station in 1952.*

46239 City of Chester *rests at Camden in 1950. It was one of the former streamlined engines and as such has a running plate without a drop-down section at the front and also has the cut away top to the smokebox. Another red backed nameplate is on show but 46231 at least had a black backed plate.*

ABOVE: *A number of A1s carried blue livery from new such as 60129 at Doncaster Works seen in June 1949. It had yet to receive its* Guy Mannering *nameplates.* H M LANE

RIGHT: *Blue had long been an established colour for the A4s on the Eastern Region but in the slightly brighter 'Garter blue' shade with red wheels. A work-worn 60005 Sir Charles Newton is seen at York in 1950 showing the lining style unique to the class. Its depot allocation is painted on the front and no doubt the class would be painted on the other side of the coupling hook.* T OWEN

BELOW: *The Eastern Region had five times the number of blue engines compared to the fleets on the Western and Southern regions with both A1s and A3s also receiving blue livery. 60065* Knight of the Thistle *carries the A3 version at Edinburgh in 1949.* J ROBERTSON

The British Railways Steam Years From 1948

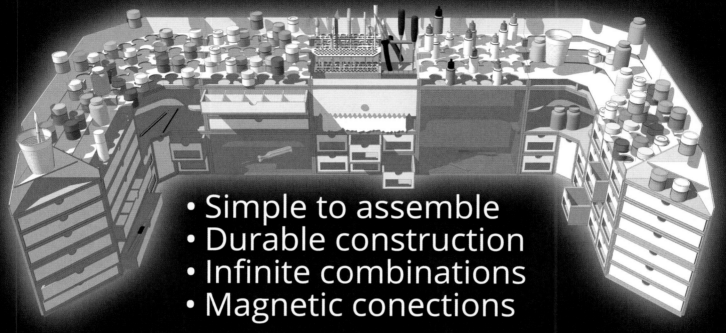
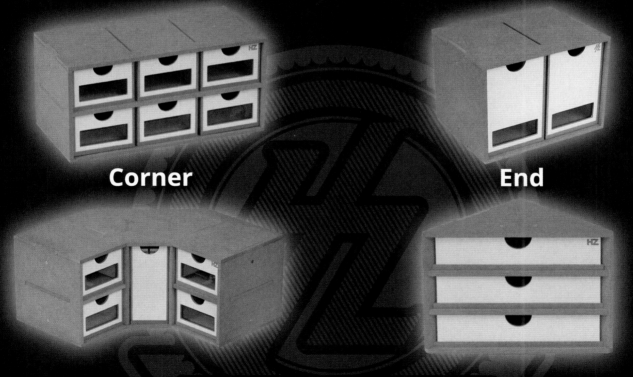

WESTERN REGION GREEN & BLACK

Following the evaluation of the views about the various trial liveries introduced in 1948, the Railway Executive set out its plans for corporate livery application early in 1949. The basics of this were the lined blue seen previously for the most powerful passenger classes, lined green (similar to that used by the GWR) for other passenger classes, lined black for the mixed traffic types and unlined black for all freight engines. All would carry a new emblem as illustrated here. This could be applied in one of two sizes, primarily dependent on the space available on the tank or tender side. Smoke box number plates were to use the same font although the numbers used on Western Region plates were an inch taller than those used elsewhere. Also, on the Western Region, some black engines had red backed nameplates.

As noted earlier, the regions started to regain some autonomy around 1955 which manifested itself most on the Western with the use of green paint on many classes, this starting to appear just before the introduction of the second BR emblem which is covered later in this volume. ∎

ABOVE: *The lion and wheel emblem introduced in 1949.*

RIGHT: *Acquired from the Cardiff Railway was 0-4-0ST 1338 seen here at Swindon in 1955. Note the application of red paint to various connecting levers - see 4358 on pages 64/65. 1338 survived long enough to receive the second BR crest at a subsequent repaint.*

The GWR inherited many tank engines from the former rail companies in South Wales. A sizable number survived into BR ownership and received unlined black livery with the first crest as shown on former Taff Vale engine 316 seen at Abercynon on June 26, 1955. T OWEN

Very few tender engines were brought into GW stock from the Welsh companies, but the Cambrian Railway did contribute some of those with 0-6-0 887 having unlined black livery with the large crest. All were withdrawn by the end of 1954; thus, none received the second crest.

The freedom to paint engines green, regardless of the use to which they were put, saw 1454 bedecked in plain green. However, it was a logical move as the most common use for the class was on passenger duties although almost always of a branch line nature. This image was captured on April 28, 1957 at Yatton. As noted previously, this class did not carry a route disc or power classification letter. T OWEN

Ever willing to bend the rules, the Western Region appeared to have decided, almost as a one-off, that 14XX tank 1411 was a mixed traffic type and was worthy of lined black livery as seen here at Banbury shed. Most of the class initially received plain black.

The 15XX pannier tanks were definitely not intended to work passenger trains but a number of the class were employed on empty stock duties at Paddington where they were very much in the public gaze. Thus, some received lined black such as 1503 seen at Old Oak Common shed on October 25, 1959. T OWEN

Almost everything is as it should be on 16XX 1662 at Swindon on March 13, 1955. Only the shed plate is missing which should be 85A for Worcester, but the engine is brand new and so the plate will probably be added when it reaches its first home. Note that the safety valve cover is painted black and only the route letter 'A' appears, no disc colour being applied as the power class was 'Unclassified'. T OWEN

Around 1956, the Western Region started to break away from the 1949 painting rules. One change was the use of green in place of black which quickly extended to include the addition of lining. 4300 class 4358 has had the full treatment here. The lining has meant that there was only room for the small crest. The Western Region had a number of works sites and Caerphilly was noted for painting the reverser rod red as seen here. Note also, the lining on the top panel of the tender, this certainly not being the norm. Swindon, 1957.

LEFT: A final example of the absorbed stock is 2168 which came from the Bury Port & Gwendraeth Railway. Again, in plain black, unlike its Taff Vale compatriot seen earlier, the small version of the crest was applied to this locomotive. This view is dated September 1955 with the engine being withdrawn in the following May.

BELOW LEFT: Given their vast numbers, the 57XX and 8750 pannier tanks showed remarkably few livery variations and very much in 'standard' dress is 3794 at Exeter St Davids on September 24, 1959, three years after the second crest started to appear. Note the black-painted safety valve cover.

BELOW: As a 'mixed traffic' type, the Saint class carried lined black livery. The 3,500-gallon tender dictated the use of the small version of the crest, the livery being enlivened by the red-backed name and number plates. A non-conformance to the standard, in this case on 2934 Butleigh Court, 82C for Swindon was the shed code number plate but the old GW code is painted below the footplate, just above the cylinder. In the background a tank engine can be seen, also carrying a red-backed number plate. T OWEN

As an express passenger class, the Stars qualified for lined green livery and **4061 Glastonbury Abbey** *carries the normal large crest. It was common when employed on Stephenson Locomotive Society rail tours for the front number plate to be removed and the buffer beam number to be reinstated as seen here. Swindon, 1955.* **T J EDGINGTON**

For a number of years neither the Grange nor Manor classes qualified for lining on their plain black livery. Seen in this unlined state is 6822 Manton Grange. Despite the 3,500-gallon tender, the large crest could be carried when there was no lining.

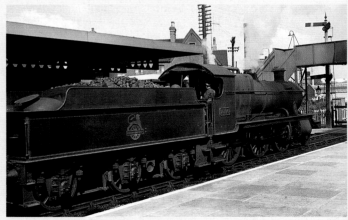

Although very much a mixed traffic type, the 43XX carried only unlined black at the outset of the new livery regime and in the case of 7306 seen here at Whitland, carried it in conjunction with the large version of the lion and wheel emblem. However, as seen on pages 64/65, on 4358, some class members later carried lined green.

ABOVE LEFT: *The full lined green style has been applied here to former GWR 4575 class 4587 seen at Brent. This included the polished safety valve cover. However, in the vcase of the 45XX class the chimney was cast iron so there was no copper cap.*

ABOVE: *Even the Western Region could not contrive to call the 2-8-0 tanks a passenger class in order for them to qualify for green paint, so the only livery carried was plain black. In this case 5232 is seen here at Neath with the large crest. As usual, the route disc is carried above the number plate.* T OWEN

LEFT: *Whilst the 57XX panniers were always painted black, one of their smaller cousins, the 54XX qualified for lined green from 1956 onwards, due to their regular passenger duties although not all received it. 5423 has the small crest carried by all of the pannier tanks, note that the lining has not been applied to the splashers.*

MAIN PICTURE: *Like the Saints, their close relative the Halls also received lined black livery. However, there are a number of differences to note compared to 2934 shown above. The size of the Hawksworth tender allowed for the use of the large crest. On the engine, 5947* **Saint Benet's Hall,** *the name and number plate background is painted black, the cylinders are not lined, and on the splashers, which have brass beading unlike the Saint, the grey band has been omitted. On the Hall the cabside lining is just a simple panel below the window but on the Saint the lining follows the cabside outline.*

Not only do liveries have to be matched to the correct period, they also have to tie in with modifications made to locomotives. A case in point was the fitting of a double chimney to some Castle class engines. The guinea pig was 7018 Drysllwyn Castle seen here at Bristol Bath Road on August 19, 1956. As it was the only Castle modified before the switch to the second crest, it is likely to have been the only one with a double chimney to run with the early crest. However, the chimney style also changed for the rest of the rebuilds and 7018 was subsequently fitted with the later pattern. T OWEN

RIGHT: *Time appears to be up for Dukedog 9011 which was put to store in the stock shed at Swindon in November 1955, being withdrawn in July 1957. The standard all-over black however has been enhanced by the yellow paint on the connecting rod. This wasn't a common embellishment, with red being the preferred colour if any rod painting was carried out.*

BELOW RIGHT: *As noted earlier, the 8750 panniers were extremely consistent in the use of unlined black livery. However, an exception was the application of lining to a small number of the class used for empty stock duties at Paddington as seen applied to 8771 on March 21, 1954. At least 8773 was similarly adorned. It would seem that the lining was not used in conjunction with the second crest.* **R BROUGHTON**

BELOW: *A number of Manor class engines went directly from plain black into full lined green as seen on 7828 Odney Manor at Shrewsbury in September 1956. In this case it included lining on the cylinder covers but not to the top panel of the tender as seen on 4358 previously.*

SOUTHERN REGION GREEN & BLACK

Ashford, Brighton and Eastleigh works were open in the period that the first crest was in use. Malachite green was phased out, followed in due course by the change from blue to green for the Merchant Navy class, the rebuilding of which started prior to the introduction of the second crest. ∎

RIGHT: *It was not known at the time that this photograph was taken that T9 30120 would be destined for stardom as the only locomotive of its kind in preservation. Since being withdrawn in 1961 in the guise of LSWR 120 it has carried a wide range of liveries but shown here at Eastleigh in April 1957, it displays standard lined black with a water cart tender carrying the small first crest. Due to the cab and splasher profiles, Southern 4-4-0 types carried a wealth of lining.*

RIGHT: *The end is nigh for G6 30349 despite the addition of the name* **Mallard** *by some local wag, it being withdrawn three months after this picture was taken. The only features worthy of mention are the small crest and the '2FB' power classification above the number.*

BELOW: *Q 30542 makes the case for the use of a larger crest, the one employed here seeming lost in an expanse of black. The Qs, despite finding employment on passenger duties, were classified as '4F' as shown on the cabside. The significance of the 'B' below the number is unknown to this writer. P HUGHES*

The 700 class of 0-6-0s carried unlined black like most of their fellows across the country. Just ex works 30699 is at Eastleigh in 1954. The loco, known appropriately as a 'black motor', carries the small crest.

As is illustrated later in the section on locomotives carrying the second crest, the 0298-class livery application varied from loco to loco. Here we have 30587 with its number on the bunker and first crest on the cabside. P HUGHES

Quite why C14 30589 gained lined black livery is a mystery as it was certainly not a passenger loco, maybe more a shed pet at Eastleigh. The layout of the number and crest has no doubt been determined by the space available.

Lord Nelson 30860 **Lord Hawke** carried the same basic lined green layout as the previously seen King Arthur, but with its larger tender had an appropriately sized crest. It is seen at Bramshott on March 2, 1957. T OWEN

ABOVE: *Lined green was the order of the day for the King Arthur 4-6-0s although the crest size looks ridiculously small. There is lining at the top and bottom of the splasher and on the running plate, the latter also continuing on the tender. It is modelled by 30805* Sir Constantine, *one of the North British built members of the class paired with a small tender at Ashford on July 23, 1953. I Davidson*

RIGHT: *A well-known but unique picture of Schools class 30915* Brighton *shows an excess of white paint applied in every conceivable place at Stewarts Lane in June 1953. However, the lined black livery was similar to that applied to the class in general although there is no lining on the cylinders and an additional red line around the cab window. There is what also looks like the Southern yellow disc on the cabside denoting water treatment, although the date seems early for this modification. D HARDY*

LEFT: *The chunky Z class tanks were never going to be graced with anything except plain black livery as seen on 30954 at Exmouth Junction on May 16, 1954. In later years the class would become synonymous with the shed but at this time 30954 was the only member of the class so allocated.* J Sutton

BELOW LEFT: *More unlined black, this time on R1 0-6-0 tank 31010 at Ashford in 1954. Unlike the Z, the R1 carries its power class stated as 2FB.*

BELOW: *Unlike the King Arthur locomotives, the Remembrance class - designated as N15X - always carried lined black despite having a power rating of 4P. Just days away from withdrawal, 32331 Beattie has been rostered for railtour duty. The lining includes the small rearmost splasher and like 30915 had a red line around the cab window. There is lining at the bottom of the tender but note the unusual treatment of the running plate lining which does not go down under the cab but continues 'straight on' to become part of the cabside lining.*

The lining on L class 31767 is best compared with the picture of T9 30120 seen earlier. The running plate lining is continued on the bottom of the tender. It is seen at St Leonards, its home shed from 1951 to 1966. **P MOFFAT**

Like the N15X, H2 Atlantic 32424 **Beachy Head** *is on railtour work at Brighton on October 5, 1952. Another passenger class that carried out its duties in lined black, it has been afforded the honour of a red backed nameplate. The cylinders are unlined.* **T OWEN**

LEFT: *A close up of the cabside of K class 32348 shows a rare use of a stencil to apply the power classification. The work has clearly just been done as the chalk line guide is still evident. May 15, 1954.* **T OWEN**

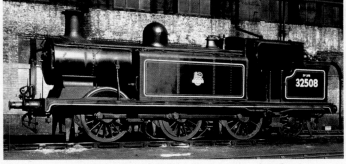

The bunker side proclaims E4 tank 32508 to have a power classification of '2P 2FB' and so it has been given lined black livery but without any boiler lining. It is seen at Brighton on April 13, 1958 where it was allocated from September 1955 until withdrawal in January 1960. **T OWEN**

There is an exception to every rule and in this case it was the application of a special livery based on Malachite green to Battle of Britain 34090 Sir Eustace Missenden Southern Railway. This included full painting of the wheels. It is seen here in February 1949, a month after entering service.

The Bulleid Leader class engines were guaranteed to break any livery scheme rules. They never got beyond the testing phase so we will never know what livery BR would have imposed on the Southern Region although lined black would have been the logical choice. As it is they were only ever seen in silver without any crest. S TOWNROE

RIGHT: *West Country Pacific 34029 Lundy carries the standard layout of lining applied to almost all Bulleid Pacifics of a black band and two orange ones with no space between the colours. They run the length of the engine and tender (when of the high sided variety) at the top and bottom with a further full depth block of black below the bottom one. The engine was one of a few West Countries that did not carry a town or city badge but the 'West Country' scroll was still placed low down to accommodate one rather than directly under the nameplate, which in this case has a black background.*

LEFT: *Q1 33034 is at Ashford on May 13, 1961 and appears to have received some minor works attention, but obviously not enough to warrant a full repaint, so four years after the introduction of the second crest it retained the earlier version at full size. To note are the two electrification flashes (and another inside the tender, rarely seen in conjunction with the first crest).*

RIGHT: *Over on the Isle of Wight things were done slightly differently. While the O2 tanks, which were the mainstay of passenger duties, received lined black livery, the E1s, whose duties were primarily freight, carried plain black and here we see W2 Yarmouth at work at Shanklin gas works. Despite the numbers always appearing in the Ian Allan publications of the day with the W prefix, the only place it was to be found was on a small plate carried on the back of the bunker as seen here.*

LEFT: *Upon rebuilding, the Merchant Navy Pacifics had a straightforward layout of the lining on the locomotive although this included the cylinders, which was unusual on the Southern. Despite having only recently been rebuilt, the engine looks care worn and faded compared to its tender which has clearly received some attention. The Merchant Navies that were rebuilt before the introduction of the second crest all seem to have run with a small version of the first one which did not suit the large tenders. That attached to 35020 Bibby Line has received an unusual livery layout with a large black panel at the top of the tender. As part of the rebuilding programme, many of the tenders were reworked to remove the high side seen here. The more normal layout can be seen on the tender to the right of the view.*

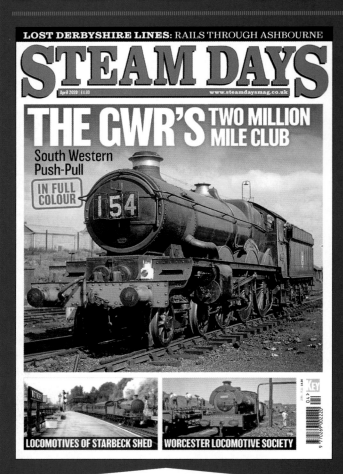

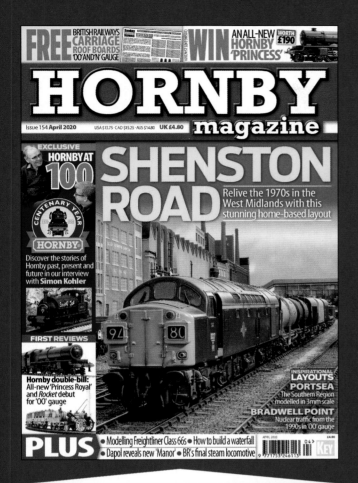

The Magazine Written by Modellers, for Modellers

Hornby Magazine takes a unique approach to model railways with both the relatively inexperienced and the seasoned modeller in mind. Unique step-by-step guides offer modellers hints and tips on how to get the most from the hobby. The very best photography and all the very latest news inspire and inform modellers of all abilities. Hornby Magazine is dedicated to promoting this most rewarding of hobbies, introducing it to newcomers and those returning to the hobby.

www.hornbymagazine.com

News, Views and Analysis on Today's Railway

Established for 50 years, Modern Railways has earned its reputation in the industry as a highly respected railway journal. Providing in-depth coverage of all aspects of the industry, from traction and rolling stock to signalling and infrastructure management, Modern Railways carries the latest news alongside detailed analysis, making it essential reading for industry professionals and railway enthusiasts alike.

www.modern-railways.com

ALSO AVAILABLE DIGITALLY:

Available on PC, Mac and Windows 10 from

181/20

FOR THE LATEST SUBSCRIPTION DEALS

VISIT:
shop.keypublishing.com

PHONE:
(UK) 01780 480404 (Overseas) +44 1780 480404

MIDLAND GREEN & BLACK

Black was the predominant engine livery colour on the LMS and subsequently on engines of LMS design, a number of which did not enter service until BR days. The only change of livery in the lion and wheel era was the abandonment of the blue paint scheme on the Pacific classes. ■

A number of 4P compounds received lined black livery as seen here on 41123 at Derby in July 1957. The boiler bands, cylinders and running plate were included in the lining scheme. **J WALLACE**

Not an image that British Railways would like to project, but life-expired engines were rarely pretty to look at and 40696 worked for only six months of its last four years in stock at Bath Green Park. It clearly took a toll on its paintwork, exposing the 'British' part of a former livery along with the more recent small crest, both applied to unlined black. Despite its recumbent state, it has at some time gained electrification flashes, not seen that often combined with the small crest.

ABOVE: *The differences in livery application on the diverse designs of class 4 tanks on the Midland are covered in more detail in the section dealing with the application of the second crest. However, here we have 42217 displaying the small crest in combination with large numbers and the power classification placed below, rather than above, the running number. There is no lining on either the boiler or cylinders.*

RIGHT: *Lined black livery was applied to the Ivatt 2MT tanks as it was to the similar BR Standard 84XXXs. 41241 retained the small crest well beyond its sell-by date as this is it in July 1963 at Crewe. Due to its longevity, electrification flashes are also carried.*

Quite how the placing and spacing of crests and numbers on 'non typical' engines was arrived at is lost in the mists of time but there is some symmetry involved with those applied to 0F 41533 seen at Staveley on March 5, 1961. There is clearly no power classification displayed.

Another ex-works view, this time of Crab 42841 at Bolton, no doubt just fresh from Horwich works for running in before returning home to Fleetwood. The black lined livery clearly includes red lines on the cylinders and as usual with a Fowler tender, the small crest is employed. T OWEN

The paint scheme applied to Princess Coronation 46221 Queen Elizabeth was identical to that on 45119 (P81) except that the Stanier tender gave room for the use of the large crest, which is seen here at Polmadie shed in September 1956. Note that the horizontal centre line of the cabside numbers coincides with that of the crest. J WALLACE

The original Patriots all ran with Fowler tenders. When lined out this dictated the use of a small crest. 45519 **Lady Godiva** passes Longsight station in June 1957. The boiler and footplate are lined but not the cylinders. W OLIVER

Sentinel designed engines were not common on BR but here we see 47181 at its regular workplace of Clee Hill, although nominally on the books of Shrewsbury shed. The positions of the crest and number are the opposite to what would be expected, possibly due to the limited space on the cabside. The date is May 14, 1956, just six months before the engine was condemned. G H HUNT

A different design of Sentinel called for a different solution. On 47190 and 47191 both the number and crest appeared as shown here except that 47191 had the positions of the crest and number transposed from those on 47190. The engine is at Crewe in April 1961, one month after withdrawal so the second crest was certainly not carried.

Ever a test for the painters, the LM Garrats were always finished in unlined black. 47972 has been given its number on both water tanks with the small crest placed on the cabside. August 26, 1956. With condemnation just eight months away it is unlikely that the second crest would ever have been applied.

ABOVE: *The Fowler 7Fs were rarely photographed in colour in part due to their early demise, but here we have 49532 displaying an unremarkable unlined black livery. The cabside power classification is absent. It is seen at Bolton on September 11, 1955 and was withdrawn before the introduction of the second crest.* T OWEN

LEFT: *Lined black livery appeared on some unlikely engines, but its use was determined by the designated power classification. The former Lancashire & Yorkshire Railway 2-4-2 tanks were designated as 2P and thus 50850 was correctly painted in lined black when seen at Newton Heath in 1961, just prior to its condemnation. Note the boiler and running plate lining and the gap in the latter underneath the cab entrance. Class mate 50865 carried continuous lining so this would appear to be due to wear or a paint 'touch up'.*

While we are nominally looking here at engines carrying the lion and wheel crest, this image gives the opportunity to study first and second crest users alongside each other. The image shows Caley 2P tanks 55219 and 55225 side by side at Corkerhill in 1958. 55219 carries the small first crest on lined black but does not have the power classification displayed. The second crest livery carried by 55255 is simply unlined black, again with a small crest but on this occasion the power classification is shown. Also note the unusual paint application to the front of Standard 4 tank 80008.

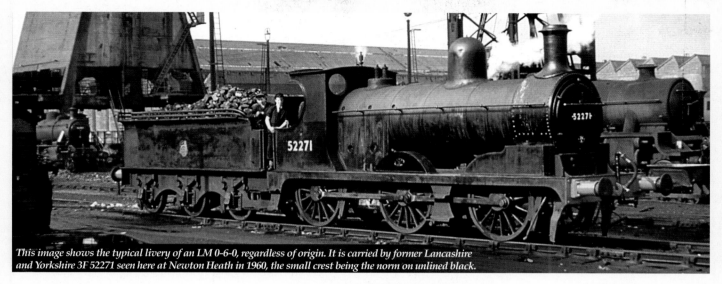

This image shows the typical livery of an LM 0-6-0, regardless of origin. It is carried by former Lancashire and Yorkshire 3F 52271 seen here at Newton Heath in 1960, the small crest being the norm on unlined black.

Showing that we are north of the border is former Caledonian Railway 3F loco 57247. Freshly attired in unlined black it does employ the 10in cabside numbers with the power classification quite high up on the cabside. A small crest adorns the tender while at the front end the shed plate has been placed above the smokebox number plate. It is at Kittybrewster on August 16, 1956. K FAIREY

With a classification of 1P it would be expected that the Johnson 0-4-4 tanks would carry lined black and indeed some class members did, but not 58066 which ended its working life at Royston shed in 1958. This was a time when, due to the substantial number of withdrawals, many engines lingered in store as did 58066 seen at Badnall Wharf in April 1959.

EASTERN GREEN & BLACK

The number of works facilities overhauling former LNER stock was considerable from Stratford in the south to Inverurie in the north. A large number of classes were also in service so a number of minor livery variations might be expected but the Eastern Region basically worked within the corporate guidelines. The only change of significance being the late (in the period) swap of livery for the V2s from lined black to lined green. ∎

For most of the period the V2 2-6-2s received lined black to replace the unlined style in which they entered BR service. Boiler and footplate lining were included but, at least on 60845 seen here at Doncaster in 1953, this did not extend to the cylinders.

RIGHT: B16/3 61448 has just emerged from Darlington works resplendent in lined black but seems to have been allocated a tender that did not require paint shop attention. The class is again painted on the buffer beam, but the allocation does not appear as a shed plate is now fitted. The cylinders are unlined.

BELOW: The A2 Pacifics did not feature in the blue painting programme. This undated picture shows 60525 A H Peppercorn at York. With the engine in the background still having 'British Railways' on its tender the most likely year is 1950. There is lining on the footplate but not the cylinders and both the class and allocation appear on the buffer beam in LNER style.

With the decision to end the use of the blue livery for classes A1, A3 and A4, all were painted lined green. Seen here is A3 60069 Sceptre at York on April 22, 1957. The large crest is evident, and the RA marking is in place at the bottom left of the cabside.

RIGHT: *In this image B17/1 61647* **Helmingham Hall** *is straight out of the paint shop at Doncaster and displaying its full lined green livery. Note that on the tender the lining is a panel only, not following the tender body profile. Lining is applied to the footplate and is continued along the bottom of the tender. The class is painted on the buffer beam, but the allocation is shown with the shed plate rather than being painted on the buffer. The small third splasher is unlined. May 12, 1956.*

This picture shows the exception to the rule. The date is October 1958, yet B17/6 61658 **The Essex Regiment** *is still in lined black with the large first crest applied. With a condemnation date of December 1959, it possibly never carried BR green livery.*

North of the border there were a number of 4-4-0 types that qualified for lined black livery. Ex North British Railway D30 62436 **Lord Glenvarloch** has a full set of additions to the basic lined black with small crest. On the cabside we have both the route availability figure and BR power classification whilst the buffer beam has the class and shed allocation despite a shed plate being in place. Boiler, splasher and footplate lining, again extended to the tender, complete the livery. P HUGHES

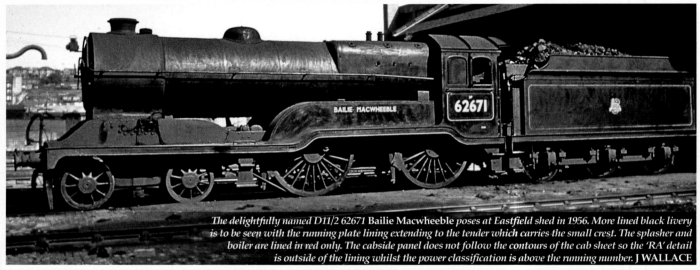

The delightfully named D11/2 62671 Bailie Macwheeble poses at Eastfield shed in 1956. More lined black livery is to be seen with the running plate lining extending to the tender which carries the small crest. The splasher and boiler are lined in red only. The cabside panel does not follow the contours of the cab sheet so the 'RA' detail is outside of the lining whilst the power classification is above the running number. J WALLACE

The British Railways Steam Years From 1948

Yet another recipient of lined black were the D49 4-4-0 locos and 62701 Derbyshire is seen at York. It has the large crest but does not carry 'RA' or power classification details on the cabside.

BELOW: *Various engines were specially cleaned prior to filming for the television programme* Railway Roundabout *and it is possible that D34s 62471* Glen Falloch *and 62496* Glen Loy *had been in receipt of the special treatment. Seen at Fort William in 1959, both have red backed number and shed plates. Additionally, 62496 has received much additional adornment to its front end including the class on the buffer beam which it might have been expected would also be on 62471 as it is on the other resident, K1 62011.*

In former Great Eastern territory at Cambridge we see D16/3 62530, again in lined black. Lining is applied to the small rear splasher on this class and below the running plate of the engine, but in this case it does not extend to the tender. The route availability is unusually placed centrally under the cabside number. The buffer beam red is extended to include the wheel guards. A number of East Anglian engines received 'special attention' and 62530 has a burnished ring on the smokebox door and polished brass on the frame of the front spectacle plate.

Q7 63462 was a recipient of unlined black and is typical of the former LNER freight engines. The large crest is carried with the only other marking being the diminutive 'RA' at the bottom right of the cab sheet. It was allocated to Tyne Dock for all of the BR period except for three years that it spent at Blaydon. The locomotive was condemned in December 1962.

ABOVE: *Providing more of a challenge for the painters is Z5 68192 in its regular haunt of Aberdeen docks. With insufficient room on the bunker or cabside the number and crest appear centrally placed on the water tank. Either the RA or power classification, we can't tell which, is placed high up on the cabside.*

LEFT: *Whilst the special painting of this J83 will have been sanctioned by a manager, the addition of a name in chalk on the side of J72 68699 will have been the work of a local comedian. Despite there appearing to be sufficient space on the bunker, the number was always placed as shown on this class. Borough Gardens shed, September 21, 1958.*

BELOW LEFT: *Among the tank classes, C16 67492 is posed at St Margaret's shed on September 13, 1957. Although somewhat grubby and apparently bufferless, the details of the lined black livery are evident. Of note are the small crest, the 'RA' at the bottom left of the side tank panel and the power classification above the number. At the front end the class and allocation appear on the buffer beam, whilst the shed and number plates are white edged. M J READE*

MAIN PICTURE: *Here we have J11 0-6-0 64427 as seen on August 26, 1956. During the BR era it was always allocated to Langwith Junction and seems to have received attention from the cleaners which is fortunate as the large crest can be seen. J SUTTON*

Another St Margaret's resident is Y9 68102, apparently in store despite appearing to be just ex-works. Despite the use of 10in numbers there is sufficient room on the cabside, and the small crest has been applied to the saddle tank. Of particular interest is the position and content of the power classification set out unusually as 0FT. The Route availability is also shown. June 6, 1952. T OWEN

The LNER had a number of 0-6-0 tanks on its books. The type seen here is a J83 68474 which had been specially painted in lined black for station pilot duties at Edinburgh Waverley. Close inspection shows that red lining was applied to the front footstep along with additional embellishments at the front end all set off with some polished brass components. August 1955. **J WALLACE**

J52/2 0-6-0T 68810 was allocated to Colwick throughout its BR life and was withdrawn in November 1955. The small crest is applied to the tank side but the position of the numbers on the cabside appear at first sight to be random as they do not fall on any obvious horizontal centre line. Unless hidden by grime, neither the RA nor power classification are carried.

Occasionally embellishments from the past survived such as this LNER plate on the cabside of Q1 69927. June 8, 1952.

Being employed regularly on passenger duties ensured that A5/1 4-6-2 tank 69808 was a recipient of lined black livery, the lining being applied beneath the running board in addition to the usual tank and cabsides but not to the boiler. The RA is applied to the bottom right corner of the water tank. It is at Boston in June 1958. A DRAKE

Apparently well cared for, despite its unlined black livery, is N1 69443 seen at Bowling shed in Bradford on April 28, 1957. It would soon be reallocated to Ardsley to see out its days. K FAIREY

BRITISH RAILWAYS STANDARD CLASSES

With the first British Railways Standard types not appearing until 1951, it would be expected that there would be full conformance with the set down livery requirements. However, with almost all railway works in the country involved in building or maintaining the engines there was always scope for minor variation. Just prior to the introduction of the second crest in 1956 regional freedom began to be exerted and in time it led to some of the Standard classes having more livery varieties than any of the engines that had originated with the 'big four'. ■

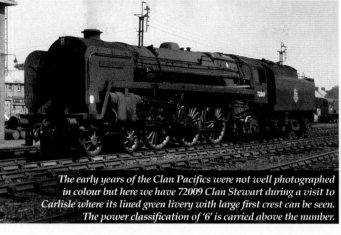

The early years of the Clan Pacifics were not well photographed in colour but here we have 72009 Clan Stewart during a visit to Carlisle where its lined green livery with large first crest can be seen. The power classification of '6' is carried above the number.

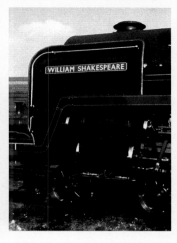

The second BR Standard type to appear was the 5MT 4-6-0 and here 73000 has arrived brand new at Neasden shed. All lining forward of the cab was applied only in red. A chime whistle was fitted at this time.

ABOVE: A Britannia pacific was displayed at the Empire Exhibition in 1951 but rather than 70000 (see below) 70004 William Shakespeare was chosen. A high gloss finish was applied to the paint work and much of the running gear and some other parts were burnished or chrome plated. It retained much of its bright metalwork when allocated to the Southern Region to work the Golden Arrow, it being the regular engine for the turn backed up by 70014 Iron Duke. Some of its bright work can be seen in this picture taken in October 1951.

70000 Britannia was the first British Railways Standard engine to enter service being allocated to Stratford shed in January 1951. However, whilst on trial from Crewe, where it was built, it did not carry lined green livery but ran in plain black and without a crest. It is seen here in standard lined green with the first crest at Stratford shed, complete with a red backed nameplate on March 23, 1958. T OWEN

ABOVE: Some members of the class destined for the Southern Region received a larger tender with extra water capacity to cover for the absence of water troughs in the area. This allowed the large crest to be used. Again, seen when new 75069 is at Swindon shed before being sent to work from Dover.

LEFT: Another brand-new engine is 2MT 78031 seen at Darlington before being allocated to Lancaster shed. The power classification is not shown and there is no running plate or cylinder lining. There is only room for the small crest.

The British Railways Steam Years From 1948

The twenty 3MT engines were constructed at Swindon although none were destined for the Western Region. 77010 was used on a running in turn which took it to Bristol. The small crest and tender lining are clearly seen. Note that the axle box covers are not picked out in yellow as seen on some second crest BR Standards.

Working through the classes we next come to the 75XXX Class 4MT 4-6-0s and a total anomaly in the shape of Swindon built 75031. Fresh from construction it carries the specified lined black livery. However, as a Swindon build the Western route disc has been added despite the fact that the engine was to be allocated to the Midland Region at Bletchley. Note the difference in the footplate lining compared to that applied to 73000. The small crest is used on this occasion. T OWEN

The 2-6-0 version of the Standard 4MT is represented by 76032. The lining layout follows that used on the 75XXX although it appears that the cylinders are unlined this time. Also note the recess on the cab for use when a tablet catcher is fitted. This may also account for the omission of the power classification. November 14, 1954 at Stratford. T OWEN

The 4MT 2-6-4 tank livery, at least as carried by 80061, has lining on the running plate but not on the cylinders and is combined with the small crest. T OWEN

The 84XXX tanks were straight forward when new, black with lining on the tank only with cabside number and power classification above. The cylinders were unlined, at least on 84010. J HILLMER

RIGHT: *Having been subjected to various renumbering schemes, the WD 2-8-0s and 2-10-0s posed few problems concerning their livery, always being plain black and carrying a large first crest. Some had the larger cabside numbers but not 90413 seen here at Lostock Hall which was its home shed from 1957 to 1961.*

BELOW: *The last Standard class to be introduced, other than 8P 71000, were the 9Fs with the first five, including 92002 illustrated here, being allocated to Ebbw Junction in January 1954. All of those put to service with the first crest were of the single chimney variety although 92002 received a double chimney later. The date is February 14, 1954 at Swindon works and the engine carries a power classification of 9F but has not yet gained a Western Region route availability disc.* **T OWEN**

THE 1956 PAINTING SCHEME
WESTERN GREEN AND BLACK

The final and longest-lasting steam engine livery change came about in 1956 with the introduction of a new crest featuring a lion holding a wheel and flanked by the words 'British Railways'. Whilst its first application was in 1956 it was not routinely applied until the middle of 1957. Its use also coincided with the loosening of the use of central guidelines as noted previously, but with the exception of the

Midland Region and a handful of engines on the Eastern, this did not spawn any new livery colours. The introduction of the new crest was not without incident as it was deemed to be a heraldic device, which required the lion to always face to the left whereas BR had planned for the lion to face forward on both sides of a locomotive. One notable change in livery application came about with the tightening of the economic screw, but also the

realisation that steam did not have long to live. This saw many engines appear without the expected lining and later without any gloss finish to their paint work. Also mentioned in this section are the application of electrification flashes, which started to be widely applied from 1961, and the painting of axle box covers in yellow, denoting that they were grease lubricated and the later addition of a red band to show that no routine lubrication was required.

On the Western Region, as noted in the section dealing with the original lion and wheel emblem, the period around 1956 heralded a new freedom in the application of liveries with the rapid re-adoption of lined green for many classes. However, the result was a plethora of livery combinations. The Western started this era with the major works of Swindon and Stafford Road but with other facilities at Newton Abbot, Caerphilly and Oswestry. By 1963 just Swindon survived for steam overhauls. ■

The second BR crest first used in 1956. It had been intended that the lion should always face the front of the engine but rules for the use of armorials require the lion to always face left and so by mid-1957 it always appeared in that way but here we have the rare 'right facing' lion.

ABOVE: 14XX 1468 bears the standard lined green carried by this class. One band of lining is carried on the boiler immediately behind the smokebox ring. The engine is at Exeter shed. S B LEE

All change on Swindon livery policy. When this image was taken it is only July 1962 but 5101 class 4110 has been deemed only to be worthy of an unlined black rather than lined, or even plain green colour scheme. It carries the large crest and the previously mentioned blue route disc.

Unlined black was the order of the day for both the 1361 and 1366 classes with the former requiring the small crest to be applied quite high up on the tank to avoid the handrail. The class did not qualify for either a route disc or power classification letter. On this occasion, in April 1960, 1361 is seen at Weymouth with a polished brass safety valve cover.

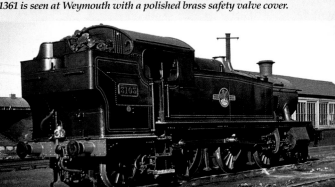

The 3100-class consisted of just five engines, although strongly related to the numerous 5101 variety of 2-6-2 tanks. 3103 must have been recently out shopped allowing it to remain in service two years longer than its class mates. It was an early recipient of the new crest and as such has the right facing lion version applied. The red route disc is below the number plate, which on this occasion is lined out. However, the 5101 class were designated as blue restriction engines rather than the red of the 31XX.

ABOVE: The County class were unique on the Western in having the straight splasher and nameplate. The lining thereon can be seen to favourable effect on 1021 County of Montgomery at Swindon shed on November 1, 1959. The large crest was standard. No shed plate is carried, but as was quite common on the Western the engine was re-allocated on completion of its overhaul and in fact was at its new home shed, having been transferred in from Laira that month. Note that the lining band on the boiler next to the firebox does not continue right around the boiler. R Patterson

RIGHT: The rough end of the steam era finds 2251 class 0-6-0 2217 at Evercreech Junction. It was moved to Somerset & Dorset territory and allocated to Templecombe shed in December 1963 lasting just 11 months before withdrawal. It would seem that lined green lies beneath the grime as this was clearly seen as late as 1962. A replacement number plate has been carefully painted but an encounter with electrification, despite the applied flashes, seems unlikely.

LEFT: *The heavy tanks such as the 5205 class were only ever destined to carry black livery seen here in conjunction with the large crest. A red route disc is carried by 5264 in the more normal position above the number plate rather than below as seen in the previous two pictures. K Nuttall*

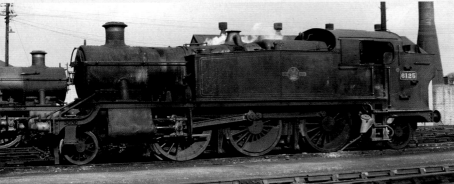

BELOW LEFT: *This 6100 class 2-6-2 tank, 6125, also carries lined green but with the small crest. It is difficult to see but at least two boiler bands are also lined but not the cylinders. Footholds were only present on the bunker on the left side of each loco but there was room for the route disc below the number rather than the standard position above. However, in this case the disc has been applied offset to the side and above the number plate.*

BELOW: *The end of BR steam was cruel to former Great Western engines. Nameplates were removed but often the supporting brackets were left in place. Those that ended up at sheds transferred to Midland Region control in 1963 also routinely had their number plates replaced with a painted version. At least on Hall 5988 Brocket Hall the numbers were applied in a neat fashion with the only green paint showing being that which had been beneath the number plate. The lined livery can just be discerned on the tender. No electrification flashes have been applied.*

The British Railways Steam Years From 1948

In complete contrast to the picture of 5988 (below left), here we see King 6006 King George I outside A Shop at Swindon Works. However, this was to be the final overhaul for the engine, and it was the first King class to be condemned in February 1962. Of note is the double red route indication and the lack of any electrification flashes. **T OWEN**

Special treatment has been afforded to 4575 class 2-6-2T 5531 seen here at Southall on March 8, 1964. Now it sports red backed number plates and front-end white paint applied to its lined green livery. Looking closely, even part of the motion appears that it might have been painted red - or is just rust? It arrived at Southall from Plymouth and lasted there just 12 months before condemnation. **K FAIREY**

Like the 54XX seen in an earlier section, the 64XX pannier tanks worked mostly passenger turns and received green paintwork. Initially this was fully lined out but even as early as 1959 the lining was not included in the repaint of at least 6426 seen at Ebbw Junction on July 12 of that year. Note that the green paintwork extended to the tank filler cap. The safety valve cover has not been painted over. **T OWEN**

Recently ex-works Grange 6863 **Dolhywel Grange** *is at its home shed of Plymouth Laira on April 29, 1962. Some of the former Great Western 4-6-0s had the 'X' seen in this view on the cabside to denote that these engines were allowed to work a load in excess of the standard set for the class. In this case electrification flashes have been added.* **J L LEAN**

When it came to the 56XX tanks there did not seem to be a set livery policy as some received green while others were consistently painted black. 6602 must have been one of the last of the class to receive works attention as the date that this image was taken is January 27, 1963. By then many of the class members had already been condemned. The large crest has been applied to the unlined black, but as seems quite common on the Western, there were no electrification flashes. **T OWEN**

ABOVE: *Great Western nameplates were very consistent in their style. Earlier we saw the exception of the straight plates fitted to the County class. When it came to some Castle locomotives that did not have 'Castle' in the title, the company resorted to adding 'Castle Class' under the name as seen here on 7007 Great Western, the final class member to be built by the company. That said, the Castles that carried 'Earl' names did not receive this treatment.* L V REASON

RIGHT: *All Halls and Modified Halls carried lined green throughout the period. Seemingly, this was without variation to the standard paint scheme apart from the previously mentioned name and number plates and the occasional addition of white paint to buffers and smokebox hinges. Modified Hall 6999 Capel Dewi Hall bursts out of Twerton Tunnel near Bath in a typical Western Region scene of the period but with Southern stock in tow on what is likely to be a Portsmouth-Cardiff duty.*

The 56XXs that did receive lined green were rarely kept as clean as Aberbeeg allocated 6644 seen here at Ebbw Junction on July 12, 1959. The two lined boiler bands can be seen along with a copper-capped chimney and polished safety valve cover. Unusually the engine carries a reporting number frame. T OWEN

Like the 2-8-0 tanks, the 7200 2-8-2 tanks only ever carried unlined black. The red route disc is clearly evident restricting them to the same routes as Castles and Halls. 7201 has just come out of the works at Swindon on October 14, 1962, this coinciding with its re-allocation from Radyr to Barry where it would survive until June 1964. The whistles have been left unpainted but as with all black engines the safety valve bonnet was painted over at overhaul. T OWEN

ABOVE: The 43XX class was another which might appear in green or black and 7340 has passed through the lined green phase to be out shopped in plain green with a large crest. A long-time resident of sheds in West Wales, it had worked as far east as Dyffryn Yard on this occasion. P HUGHES

RIGHT: Unlined black was again the order of the day, this time on the 94XX tanks with an unusually clean 8420 showing this off at Old Oak Common on September 26, 1963. At this time there was a rapid turnover of engines used for ECS duties into Paddington and no doubt 8420 was kept clean for that job. Note that the number is also chalked on the side of the smokebox and the route colour is red.

RIGHT: : Like the passenger classes, the last surviving ex Great Western tank engines were allocated to sheds latterly under the control of the Midland Region. This resulted in the removal of number plates with painted numbers substituted. Although looking very run down, 0-6-0PT 8718 at least had its number painted in Great Western style when seen at Halesowen in February 1966. R SIVITER

The British Railways Steam Years From 1948

SOUTHERN GREEN AND BLACK

While the Southern Region had the smallest fleet of steam engines, it was comprised of a relatively large number of classes, and variations could also arise where different tender types could be found within one class. The choice of liveries was lined green and both lined and unlined black, and there was consistency of application for most of the time as on the closure of the Ashford and Brighton works, all repairs were undertaken at Eastleigh. ■

RIGHT: Unlined black adorns S15 30508 at Eastleigh shed in 1963. The eight-wheel tender provides ample room to apply the larger size totem. The only other item of note is the single electrification flash.

Another freight type was the massive H16 2-6-4 tank, of which 30520 was an example. With the large tank size, it was possible that a larger logo could have been used but not in this case. The height of application appears to be matched by that of the running number. As with the engines depicted on these pages, the power classification is carried above the running number.

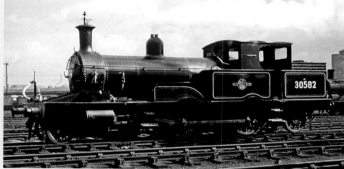

Loved by enthusiasts, the Adams radial tanks were usually kept in clean condition to display their lined black livery to good effect. 30582 has gone up to London for railtour duties. The boiler and cylinders are lined but electrification flashes seem to have passed it by. DAVID A LAWRENCE

Cleaned up especially for a railtour was M7 30107, thus allowing us to see the full extent of the lined black livery, typical of that applied to the range of Southern tanks that were employed on passenger duties. The burnished or painted smokebox straps were unusual on a tank and on this occasion the number plate possibly has a green background, but that may just be the light playing tricks. The engine is at Dorchester West on June 7, 1958. T OWEN

Lord Nelson class 30856 **Lord St Vincent** has just come out of the paint shop at Eastleigh on September 18, 1960. Like 30788 (opposite page) it has lining along the bottom edge of the tender. The cylinders and boiler are also lined. Note the dip in the lining on the centre splasher to accommodate the nameplate. Also, for the 'St' in St Vincent the Southern have used a small sized capital T after the S and there is no full stop. T OWEN

Representative of some of the old 4-4-0 types operating on the Southern is T9 30707 and as a passenger type it received lined black livery. Note the lining applied both to the wheel splashers and to those for the rods. A large totem has been used on this occasion. Eastleigh shed, August 21, 1960.

N class 31413 enjoyed the use of lined black livery which can be seen to be extended along the running plate in this view taken at Eastleigh on May 25, 1963. The slacker pipe unfortunately covers part of the power classification and might also cover the water treatment symbol if there is one. However, we can discern that the large emblem is carried. R TIBBITS

All three members of the 0298 class are lined up at Nine Elms on December 15, 1962, returning to their old operating territory to work a farewell railtour. It can clearly be seen that 30586 has its number and crest in the opposite positions to its classmates, whilst there also seems to be a slight inconsistency in the placing of the number and crest on the other two class members as well. G PARRY COLLECTION

ABOVE: The Schools class 4-4-0s were a bit of a nightmare when it came to liveries as several retained variations of black livery until the end in the 1960s and yet it would have been expected that by that time they would have been green. Here we see 30901 **Winchester** just months before condemnation at Stewarts Lane shed on August 8, 1962. Observe that whilst the engine does not carry running plate lining, the 'bottom of tender' orange line is present, and yet it stops short of the tender steps. Also, the lining on the cab is not continuous. A water treatment yellow circle is carried below the number. This is explained more in the section on the BR Standards. The whole is set off by a red-backed nameplate whereas the Lord Nelson seen previously has a black backed plate.

A rear view of King Arthur 30770 **Sir Piranius** reveals that lining was carried at the very bottom of the side of the eight-wheel tender to match that on the locomotive running board. The large logo is employed. This picture was taken on September 2, 1962, just two months before the locomotive's withdrawal. **A F HUDSON**

C class 0-6-0s carried out some of the limited mundane freight duties on the Southern although they did find occasional use on passenger duties but only ever warranted unlined black. No power class is to be found on 31692. Also, on a more general note this engine, like most seen so far on the Southern, has not got any electrification flashes. March 12, 1960 at Hither Green. T OWEN

Comparison should be made here with the earlier view of T9 30707 to see how the lined black livery was adjusted to blend in with the varying design lines of the Southern 4-4-0s. Here we have L class 31778 at Brighton. As with the three green engines seen so far, the footplate lining is extended to the tender. P HUGHES

ABOVE: U class 31790 appears a little care worn but the application of its lined black livery is evident and is once again continued along the bottom of the tender which has the small crest. On the cabside we have an extended power classification of 4P 5F and placed to the right, rather than in a central position, is the water treatment triangle which replaced the circle seen on the Schools. This engine does have electrification flashes and is at Guildford on May 1, 1964. A F HUDSON

RIGHT: Here we have a most unusual application of the number and crest on E2 class 32108 with both being placed on the tank side and not quite at the same height. This possibly has something to do with the white plate fitted to the bunker, these usually noting some experiment being carried out on the particular engine although there appears ample room to apply the number on the bunker as was done on the rest of the class. The image was taken in June 1958 at Southampton docks. W BOYDEN

Another class afforded lined black mixed traffic livery were the Ks with ex works 32338 featuring at Ashford on October 11, 1959. Note that the number and shed plates have been painted over.

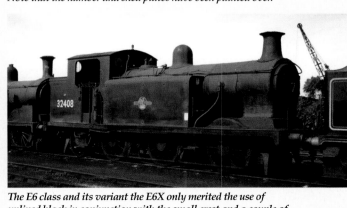

The E6 class and its variant the E6X only merited the use of unlined black in conjunction with the small crest and a couple of electrification flashes. 32408 is at its home shed of Eastleigh on August 4, 1962 and would be condemned at the year end.

The rebuilding of the Bulleid West Country and Battle of Britain classes did not begin until 1959 so fortunately variations in livery are rare. Here 34009 *Lyme Regis* appears to have received some minor attention as some paint work is cleaner than the rest. Despite the year being 1963 when this image was taken, no electrification flashes have been fitted. On the cabside we have a power classification of 7P 5FA and a water treatment triangle. The red-backed nameplate was the norm but not present on all of the class. M CHAPMAN

Nameplate styles varied more on the Southern than on the other regions. Here we see a typical King Arthur plate from 30782 **Sir Brian,** that from West Country 34001 **Exeter** following rebuilding (note the black background on this occasion) and Battle of Britain 34066 **Spitfire** which is unusually painted red instead of the more usual light blue. Finally, we see the cabside crest affixed to 34067 **Tangmere.** Another engine to carry extra cabside adornment was 34050 **The Royal Observer Corps.** R PATTERSON AND T OWEN

Perhaps the most diminutive engines to be awarded lined black status were the A1X Terrier tanks whose duties were mainly on branch line passenger work. As can be seen in this picture, there were two lining and numbering schemes employed depending on the size of the bunker as these varied between engines. Both the course of the lining and the size of the numbers had to be adjusted to suit. 32670 and 32646 show off the variants at Eastleigh shed on May 22, 1960. R PATTERSON

On the Isle of Wight corporate guidelines were followed except that the crest had to be placed above the nameplate rather than on the centreline of the tank. Lined black was superseded by economy black for a few of the O2 tanks in the dying days of steam. The island fleet were maintained and overhauled at Ryde throughout and the nominal 'W' prefix to the numbers never appeared except on a plate on the bunker. Seen here is 21 **Sandown.** G S COCKS

The paint scheme of the rebuilt Merchant Navy class appeared identical to that employed for the West Country and Battle of Britain rebuilds. However, 35027 **Port Line** carries a black-backed nameplate and 8P power classification. Eastleigh, January 1958.

*Due to the unusual nature of the original 7P Pacifics, a modified lining was applied as standard and as seen here on 34055 **Fighter Pilot** consisted of orange and black for the full length of the boiler side at both the top and bottom of the air smoothed casing. Black paint was applied for any metal work below the bottom band on the engine. A SAINTY*

The British Railways Steam Years From 1948

MIDLAND GREEN AND BLACK

Former LMS engines continued with either green or black paint schemes from the 1956 crest change until the end of BR steam with one planned and one unplanned deviation from the corporate rules. Derby works ceased steam overhauls sometime before the end of steam as did Horwich works leaving just Crewe and Glasgow to overhaul and repaint the diminishing fleet. ∎

The first deviation from the corporate livery scheme was very much unplanned and was a complete 'one off' which saw 4P compound 41101 painted in red and yellow to work an Andy Capp special to Blackpool on September 8, 1959. It is thought not to have done any other work painted in this way and was soon parked on the scrap road at Derby and despatched with haste.

To every rule there is an exception and you could view a multitude of pictures of Ivatt 2MT tanks and miss the fact that 41314 was indeed an exception. The normal lining plan for the class saw them with an unlined bunker but this loco has it fully lined along with the boiler and cylinders and in addition it has the mighty power classification of 2P/3FA applied to the cabside. It has electrification flashes although the chance of it reaching the overhead lines from its home at Barnstaple must have been quite slim.

FAR LEFT: 0F 41537 posed few problems to the painters in deciding where to place the number and crest - little more can be said on this occasion! It is seen here at Gloucester on March 23, 1963 and despite its near pristine condition, it would be withdrawn six months later.

LEFT: Unlike the previously mentioned 41537, the Class 4 tanks of the three distinctive designs provided plenty of variety despite the fact that they only ever carried black in lined and unlined versions. Fairburn designed 42082 shows the standard lining for its type although showing the power classification of 4P rather than 4 or 4MT and has the early 'right facing' lion.

On the Fowler designed engines there was plenty of room for lining below the running plate as seen here on 42334 at Wellingborough on August 20, 1961. As on the Stanier design (see the following illustration) the buffer beam red did not extend up as far as the running plate. Three electrification flashes can be seen.

Just as it should be, although Crabs rarely appeared in anything like as clean a state as this. 42816 at Horwich displays the small crest, full running plate, cylinder and boiler lining with the simple '5' power classification. P Hughes

On the Stanier version of the design the running plate was of sufficient depth to allow the lining to be continued to the front of the engine, otherwise there is little to choose between them except that 42536, seen here at Derby on August 29, 1957, employs a non-standard font for its front number plate. This image helps us date the change to a left facing lion. A number of the class later succumbed to unlined black.

RIGHT: *The use of 'economy black' on Stanier 5MTs made life simple as it seems to have been applied in a consistent style at Crewe. The variety this time is provided by the engine, 44765, which is fitted with a double chimney. It was allocated to Crewe throughout its BR life but is seen here at Willesden on May 12, 1965. The presence of roller bearings on the tender is highlighted by the yellow-painted axlebox covers.*

BELOW: *Not much livery to see here, as we cannot determine if the grime hides lined or unlined black, but 44899 does illustrate how a modeller could portray the end of BR steam so of note we have the minor detail of white painted bolts on the number plate, a crudely hand painted '10F' shed allocation in lieu of a plate and the contradictory 'Carlisle Kingmoor' allocation on the buffer beam, all matched with a miniature snow plough. The '10F' allocation dates the picture to between January and July of 1968.*

Things have become much less elaborate on classmate 42938 unless the grime is hiding the lining as it appears to simply have a lined cabside and is paired with an unlined tender. It is at Hellifield on September 8, 1962. At least one electrification flash has been applied on the rear of the tender.

Apparently past its sell-by date, 4F 44278 rests at Westhouses. This 4F is paired with a 'tender cab' and survived long enough to require the application of the cabside stripe, being withdrawn in January 1966. A small crest and two electrification flashes complete the picture.

RIGHT: The Stanier version of the Lancashire and Yorkshire 2-6-0 design has a lined tender and cabside. The boiler and cylinders appear to be plain black, but there is a possibility that the running plate has lining under the grime. Once again, the small crest has been applied along with the '5' power classification. 42951 was a Nuneaton engine at this time but has ambled to Willesden where it was photographed on August 29, 1964.

BELOW: Some of the Ivatt 4MTs were graced with lining but 43061, seen here at Doncaster on April 10, 1960 is already being consigned to an existence in unlined black. The small crest is matched with 10in numbers. Note that a tablet catcher is fitted at this time.

Unlined black on a Midland 4F should be a simple thing to get right. However, this particular 4F was one of a few allocated north of the border and ended up at Fort William as their snow plough engine, hence the unusual tender. 44255 appears to have also had the attention of the Scottish painters as it has large cabside numerals and a power classification of '4F' combined with the unusual (for the class) large totem.

Another 'end of steam' view but at least Jubilee 45596 Bahamas was looked after by its home shed of Stockport. It survived with lined green livery until the end but at some point had a tender swap with an unlined and small crested compatriot. The 'not south of Crewe' yellow stripe has been applied along with a hand painted name and a red-backed front number plate.

Another plain green member of the class at the end was 45697 **Achilles** which like **Bahamas** had a tender swap but on this occasion it was a lined black example that was provided. The yellow stripe is present and apparently a painted name when seen at Kettlebeck in April 1967. The engine lasted just long enough to see out the summer timetable, being withdrawn in the September.

LEFT: A number of the Jubilees allocated to Carlisle and Corkerhill were paired with a Fowler tender and thus carried the small tender emblem. Many also seem to have been maintained at Glasgow works and so had the large cabside numbers. Much more rarely photographed than their southern based cousins, many were withdrawn as early as 1962. Here we see 45715 **Invincible** which was condemned in December of that year.

Scot 46156 **The South Wales Borderer** is seen at Cricklewood on October 12, 1963, a date which coincides with its transfer from Willesden to Annesley. Close inspection of the picture seems to show that only two boiler bands are lined and there is no lining on the cylinders, but it is present on the running board. Also, only the front and rear splashers are lined in orange.

Remembered by some is the 1960s Hornby model of a Princess Coronation or Duchess which depicted 46232 **Duchess of Montrose.** Here we see it ex works at Crewe on March 15, 1959 and there can be no doubt about the placing of the lining in this side view. All of the Duchesses allocated north of the border and some English based examples remained in green although on occasions they received a background colour to their nameplates.

BELOW: *The Midland Region, like the Western, decided to show some links to its past by repainting some of its Pacifics into what has been described variously as red, crimson lake and maroon. Whatever your preference the engines certainly stood out from the crowd. Princess 46207 Princess Arthur of Connaught is seen at Camden so adorned in August 1961. Note that the red was applied to both the cylinders and front steps. However, lining was not applied to the boiler.*

BELOW RIGHT: *Unlined green did little to enhance the Jubilees and fortunately few of them suffered the fate but one that did was 45675 Hardy. It appears to still have its original nameplate fitted and only the flashes relieve the green as a yellow stripe has yet to be applied.*

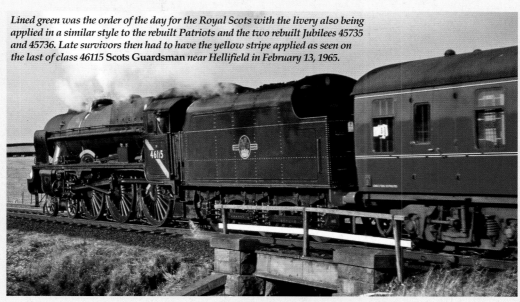

Lined green was the order of the day for the Royal Scots with the livery also being applied in a similar style to the rebuilt Patriots and the two rebuilt Jubilees 45735 and 45736. Late survivors then had to have the yellow stripe applied as seen on the last of class 46115 **Scots Guardsman** *near Hellifield in February 13, 1965.*

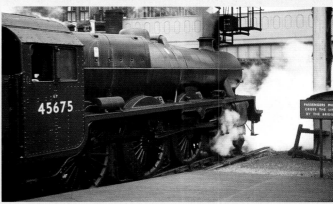

Jubilee 45660 **Rooke** *all present and correct in lined green at Camden on March 31, 1962, although it will have raised a few eyebrows as it was allocated to Shrewsbury at the time.*

ABOVE: *A handful of Duchesses carried the coat of arms applicable to their namesake above the nameplate, one such being 46254* City of Stoke-on-Trent, *note the use of hyphens in the name.* T OWEN

LEFT: *46256* Sir William A Stanier F R S *is immaculate at Crewe in April 1962. It and fellow 46257* City of Salford *had the revised cab side sheet profile and also roller bearings, their presence being highlighted by the yellow/red striped axlebox covers. There were two versions of the red livery with just a couple of engines receiving the first type which appeared to use a slightly lighter shade of red and yellow lining rather than the later gold/cream shade seen here.*

LEFT: *One 'Jinty' 3F 47482 outshone its brethren by at one time having its number applied to the middle of the tank side instead of on the bunker like all of the others. At the time it was allocated to Crewe and was on occasions used as the station pilot which might explain the break from the rules. Electrification flashes are carried.*

The British Railways Steam Years From 1948

BELOW RIGHT: *The 47XXX 0-4-0STs came in two designs. 47000-4 were such that the crest could be easily applied to the tank. However, at least on 47005 of the second batch it has been placed alongside the number. Perhaps, as the power classification was '0' it was decided not to put it on the engines. Staveley, December 1963.*

RIGHT: *Plain black was always the order of the day for the Stanier 8F class so livery variants were not too common. However, occasionally a small number of the class were paired with a Fowler tender such as 48755 seen here at Lancaster in 1962. This one then carried the small version of the crest rather than the large version associated with the usual Stanier designed tender.* **M CHAPMAN**

Stanier 8F normality, well almost. 48773, one of the three members of the class that were withdrawn early by the Scottish Region and subsequently re-instated on the Midland Region, was wrongly given the yellow stripe treatment. Seen on an 'end of steam' railtour job it has also acquired a painted 'shed plate'. **A GRAY**

After the brightness of the red Duchesses we return to the more mundane unlined black applied to Ivatt 2MT 46468. Although starting life allocated in England, it moved north of the border in 1961 where it was repainted using the large numbers and crest. No power classification has been applied. The class had carried many livery combinations, in the main due to the fact that some were allocated to the Western Region and were painted green as well as lined black. See also the similar 78XXX examples.

BELOW RIGHT: *Representing the Caledonian Railway stock is 3F 56239 which appeared to be ex-works when photographed at Polmadie on May 18, 1959. Unlined black was the norm for the freight classes north of the border as it was for the rest of the country. The number is applied at standard size but is not at the same height as the crest, the latter being one of the rare 'facing forward' variety. Red connecting rods are a distinctive feature, brass oil fillers also appear along with either a gold painted or polished brass works plate.*

RIGHT: *This picture shows the battered state of the Westinghouse pump on 3F 56347, possibly caused by the legendary 'hit with a spanner' technique to make it work. However, we can also see that 56347 has carried its number in two positions and in two sizes with the former 5 and 3 showing through under the existing paintwork.*

BELOW: *Concluding our look at former LMS power we see 57689 at Stirling shed. As a freight engine it is again in unlined black with a small crest but large numbers. The unusual feature for a freight type is the Scottish blue background to the number plate and it also has its 66B shed plate affixed in an unusual position, this also possibly having a blue background. Two electrification flashes are evident, one unusually being placed on the cab sheet.*

Another 'always black' class were the LNWR 0-8-0s. Seen just days before withdrawal in December 1964, 48895 rests at Bescot shed complete with the yellow stripe. Along with the 589XX coal tanks and the engines on the Isle of Wight the LNWR 7Fs were unique in being the only large classes of engine not to be fitted with a front number plate.

EASTERN GREEN AND BLACK

On engines of LNER origin the introduction of the second crest was a straightforward affair although with all of Doncaster, Darlington, Stratford, Gorton and the Scottish Region works involved there was scope for the usual minor variations. The Eastern Region also indulged in a small number of 'independence' liveries. ■

ABOVE: *Some members of the A4 class carried a coat of arms or other embellishment associated with their name. Illustrated here is 60009* Union of South Africa *with its cabside crest. Another such was 60011* Empire of India *while 60027* Merlin *carried a badge on the left side of the boiler. 60022* Mallard *had its speed record plaques mounted in the same position but on both sides whilst 60010* Dominion of Canada *carried a front mounted bell for a number of years.* P HUGHES

RIGHT: *Proving that nothing to do with liveries is straightforward is this picture of 60112 St. Simon on railtour duty at Waterloo on August 25, 1963. As can be seen, the engine is in unlined green and appears to be unique amongst Eastern Pacifics in that respect, but it is paired with a lined green tender. The route availability is shown in the standard position on the cabside and at least one electrification flash is carried.* A F HUDSON

Engines working the crack expresses on the Eastern Region were noted for their elevated level of cleanliness which extended to burnished buffers and cylinder covers to compliment the lined green livery. On this occasion A4 60028 Walter K Wigham *has been taken one stage further with the application of white paint to the cab roof, an honour only extended to engines that worked royal trains. This picture dates from June 1961.* J F AYLARD

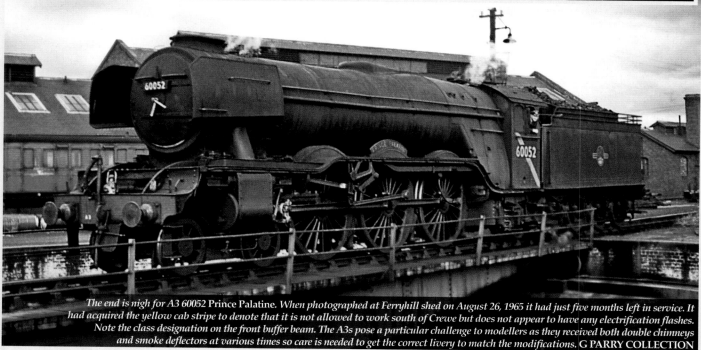

The end is nigh for A3 60052 Prince Palatine. *When photographed at Ferryhill shed on August 26, 1965 it had just five months left in service. It had acquired the yellow cab stripe to denote that it is not allowed to work south of Crewe but does not appear to have any electrification flashes. Note the class designation on the front buffer beam. The A3s pose a particular challenge to modellers as they received both double chimneys and smoke deflectors at various times so care is needed to get the correct livery to match the modifications.* G PARRY COLLECTION

LEFT: *Scottish Region allocated A1 60161* North British *shows off its full lined green livery including that along the running plate, but none on the cylinders. Local pride has seen the nameplate background painted red along with burnished buffers and smoke box straps.* **J ROBERTSON**

BELOW: *A small number of A2 Pacifics became unusual residents of Polmadie shed in 1963 where they appeared to do little work. Condemnation for 60535* Hornet's Beauty *came in June 1965 and it was still there in the middle of July. The grime covers much of its lining but on the cabside the yellow stripe has been applied, partially covering the 'RA' designation.*

For many years lined black was the standard livery for the B1 4-6-0s. B1 61119 has got lining on the running plate but does not seem to have any on the boiler bands or cylinder covers but has acquired a large quantity of 'bull' at March shed, even extending to painted wheel rims, but no 'RA' is carried on the cabside. The picture is dated May 30, 1963 and the engine was withdrawn from service six months later. **D PRESTON**

ABOVE: *The V2 2-6-2s were one of the classes that moved from black to green livery. In this image 60836 stands at Tweedmouth on April 23, 1966 resplendent in lined green. It has electrification flashes but no 'RA' on the cab nor a class shown on the buffer beam which appears to have been repainted in a non-standard shade of red. Whilst not a livery variation, a number of Scottish V2s acquired a bent handrail on the smokebox door, the reason suggested being that it was used to suspend lifting tackle when working on the inside cylinder.*

RIGHT: *The B16 4-6-0s were a class that rarely attracted the attention of the cleaners so often it is not easy to see if they were in lined or unlined black livery as both were used. However, here 61435, seen at Darlington in May 1963, appears to be not long out of the works and so the detail of its lined black livery is clear. It shows that neither cylinder lining nor the 'RA' detail have been applied but electrification flashes are present.* P HUGHES

ABOVE: *Another of the rare right facing lions is to be found on the tender of K4 61995* **Cameron of Lochiel** *when photographed at Crianlarich on June 18, 1960. The lined black livery can be clearly seen and on this occasion includes both the power classification set out as 5MT. (note the full stop), the route availability and a blue backed nameplate. F Hornby*

LEFT: *Both B2 and B17 4-6-0s carried lined green with the large second crest. Note that the lion in the crest on B17/1 61620* **Clumber** *is facing right. As stated in the introduction it was ruled that the logo was a heraldic device and as such the lion should always face left and quite soon after its use commenced, this ruling was enforced. Note that some members of this class used colour-backed nameplates. P HUGHES*

ABOVE: *Railtours could be useful in that on many occasions the locomotives concerned were given special attention by the cleaners. That is likely to have been the case for D34 4-4-0 62471 Glen Falloch when employed as such at Greenlaw in April 1959. The large crest is employed on the lined black livery with both the power classification and RA information applied. Careful inspection of the picture suggests that red paint was used between the frames. The white edged number plate was a feature on a number of Scottish engines.*

RIGHT: *The painting of K1 62005 is almost certainly the work of the Master Neverers Association, a group of enthusiasts who worked clandestinely at sheds to clean engines before they went to take photos of them in action. The application of a mock copper-capped chimney is perhaps taking things a little too far. The base livery was lined black.* P HUGHES

Q6 63395 shows off the simplicity of unlined black with the large crest. Nothing denotes the power classification or route availability with the number being placed quite high on the cabside. Electrification flashes complete the scene along with brass oil pots. R OAKLEY

North of the border we have J37 64599 again showing off its plain black livery. This time the tender displays the small crest while the cabside number appears to have been applied at the same height. Other than electrification flashes there are no distinguishing marks. P Hughes

Another interpretation of BR black. This time the large crest has been chosen for J21 65033 with the cabside number applied halfway up the side so not lining up with the tender crest. Although on freight duties it is believed this picture dates from a period when 65033 was used on a railtour. That probably accounts for the polished brass safety valves as well as the brass band fitted immediately behind the smokebox. Newcastle 1960.

Although 63395 was nicely clean, O2/3 63948 positively sparkles being straight from the paint shop at Doncaster. This time the number is on the centreline of the cab and the route availability is shown but not the power classification. On the buffer beam the class appears simply as 'O2'. P Hughes

The challenges of painting tank engines in the corporate style appear here with the J94s, where the decision to place the small crest above the number centrally on the tanks seems logical on 68047. No other markings appear. Remarkably 68064 a long-time resident of Gorton shed, had the number, in large numerals, placed high up on the side of the bunker.

As with the Western Region, tank engines employed on duties that brought them to the attention of the public sometimes received 'special treatment'. J69/1 68619 was the resident pilot engine at London Liverpool Street station and acquired Great Eastern Railway's very dark blue livery with a lot of lining out and even red coupling rods and a GER coat of arms. May 23, 1961. T OWEN

RIGHT: York and Newcastle Central were two further locations where special liveries were to be seen, in both cases applied to J72 0-6-0Ts. Apple green was the base colour but with BR style lining which was applied additionally to the buffer beam and steps. The BR and company crests were placed either side of the loco number. 68736 rests at York. P HUGHES

BELOW: J50 0-6-0 tanks did not meet the public so often and were all in plain black livery. The exact position of the number and crest varied with the latter in this case placed simply to avoid the weld on the tank side. One valve below the running plate seems to have attracted red paint on J50/3 68985 at Doncaster in September 1959. C J B SANDERSON

The N7 0-6-2 tank class was frequently used on passenger duties and thus it appeared in lined black livery as modelled by N7/3 69675 at Stratford on September 19, 1959. Many of these engines were kept in immaculate condition by their crews with occasional embellishments. Note the use of red paint between the frames and the brass oil pots. T OWEN

THE BR STANDARD CLASSES

The British Railways Standard types were anything but standard when it came to livery variations. They were at the mercy of all of the BR workshops, each of which had their own ideas on the application of corporate liveries. Britannia 70016 became the first engine to carry the second emblem, this being applied in June 1956, but it was to be well into 1957 before it was used as standard on repainting. The WD locomotives are included here for completeness. ∎

LEFT: *In the final years of BR steam, nameplates were removed from most locomotives including the* Britannia *class. Some enthusiasts and even shed staff then took matters into their own hands and painted the name on or made wooden replicas for some engines. In happier times, whilst the standard background colour for* Britannia *nameplates was black, examples ran with both (Scottish) light blue and red plates. 70015 and 70026 display painted names at Stockport.*

RIGHT: *70013* Oliver Cromwell *was the last of its class to be put through Crewe works for overhaul and was subsequently chosen by BR to be the engine used on the final steam railtours. It appeared in lined green but often ran without its nameplates. Electrification flashes were carried and the covers on the roller bearing axles were painted yellow. Prior to this a number of the class were turned out in 'economy' unlined green such as 70034 seen further on in this section. Some former Western Region engines continued to carry their route disc on lined green.*

LEFT: *70034, formerly Thomas Hardy, shows off a very dull 'economy green' at Carlisle Kingmoor. As well as omitting the lining, either limited quantities of, or no varnish at all seems to have been used. Only one electrification flash is evident compared to the three on 70013 and it is unlikely that the axlebox covers were ever yellow.*

BELOW: *At least with 8P 71000* Duke of Gloucester *there was little scope for confusion with its liveries as standard lined green with both first and second crests was used and the later addition of electrification flashes. It is seen here at Camden in June 1962.*

Like 71000, the liveries carried by the 6MT Clan class were uncomplicated. Other than the two crest variants and electrification flashes, other things to be aware of are the use of coloured backed nameplates, as seen here on 72006 **Clan Mackenzie** at Crewe South and the incorrect addition of the yellow cabside stripe as the restriction did not apply to the class. At least two of 72000 to 72004 went for scrap without ever carrying the second crest.

Twenty of the Southern Region Standard 5MTs received names, this process starting in 1958. 73089 **Maid of Astolat** carries lined black with the nameplate covering the red lining. The cylinders are lined in red and the axlebox covers are yellow even as late as August 1963, no electrification flashes were carried by this engine. The Southern was the recipient of many members of the class from other regions so a number of minor variations could be enjoyed.

At least one 75XXX 4-6-0 succumbed to unlined black, even briefly covering the number plate. 75009 has just been so adorned at Crewe Works. The minimal shine on the paintwork is evident. A small crest is carried but no power classification.

Once resplendent in full lined green, Standard 5MT 73095 has been downgraded to the dull economy version. Although it is difficult to tell under a layer of grime, the power classification does not appear to be painted on the cabside, nor is it obvious if the running plate is painted green or black. One electrification flash can be seen along with the yellow axlebox covers on the tender. Taken at Croes Newydd shed on March 3, 1966.

The grime may also be hiding the truth in this view of Standard 5MT 73101 at Kingmoor shed. It certainly carries the large numbers typical of engines overhauled in Scotland and is painted black. One is tempted to say that it is unlined, but closer inspection of the cabside appears to show lining under the filth. Whilst it was normal to show the power classification as '5' on the Midland, Scottish authorities have applied it as '5MT'

75047 displays a version of lined black as applied to many of the class. However, note that there is no lining on the boiler or cylinders and even although this picture dates from August 20, 1966, there do not appear to be any electrification flashes fitted. The clean livery is enhanced by the addition of white paint and a red-backed number plate at the front end. **T OWEN**

LEFT: *The 2-6-0 version of the BR Standard 4MT qualified for lined black livery and 76088, seen at Cricklewood on May 19, 1963, displays the full version with lined boiler bands and cylinders. Later members of the class were built after the introduction of the second crest and so would not have carried the lion and wheel version. The power class is correctly shown as just '4' and two electrification flashes can be seen. The large crest was carried by some of the class that were paired with the high sided tender.*

The 75XXX class was one of the most confusing when it comes to livery variants, due in part to their use on the Western Region which then proceeded to paint them in various styles of green. However, 75016 in lined green is a bit of a mystery engine as it was never allocated to the Western, the nearest it got being at Shrewsbury shed after it became part of the Midland Region. This view of it at Eastleigh was taken in July 1964. Despite the lined green it does not carry a WR route disc (it was allocated to Nuneaton at this time). The axlebox covers here have a red band on yellow. Despite this quite late paint date, just two years later it had visited a works again and been repainted in plain green.

Standard 3MT 77012 has been relegated to unlined black, the class having run for most of the time in lined black. With the lining left off, the large crest has been applied but the power classification on the cabside has been omitted. The tender axlebox covers are yellow beneath the grime and three electrification flashes are evident on the tender.

The influence of the Western Region is evident within the 78XXX Standards although only the first ten had an allocation there. As early as August 1961, 78000, seen at Aberystwyth, had reverted from lined to unlined green but with the large crest. Just visible is the GW style route disc on the cabside. T OWEN

The use of lining dictated the application of a small crest on 78004. The boiler bands and cylinders are also lined. Unusually for a Western engine the power classification appears on the cabside rather than the route disc. No electrification flashes have been applied. Gloucester, April 13, 1962.

Standard 4MT tank 80010 was the first of the class to run, this being in July 1951. September 1957 saw it freshly painted at Eastleigh and now carrying the second crest with the full lining evident. No power classification is carried but there is what, at first sight, might be thought to be a WR route disc above the number. This symbol was in fact to denote that water treatment was fitted to the engine and was only carried by Southern Region based engines. The Western soon requested that the symbol be changed to prevent confusion with its disc system and the Southern replaced it with a triangle.

80095 displays yet another set of variations. As a Southern example it carries the water treatment symbol, still a circle in this case, but now it is below the number with the single '4' as the power classification above the number. Just one electrification flash appears to be applied to the bunker, this being in a central position. For those interested in liveries, the container on the first wagon may enliven the scene. G PARRY COLLECTION

The British Railways Steam Years From 1948

84025 as turned out from Ashford works. There were three livery changes from the 84000-19 batch, large cabside numbers, no power classification and a variance to the lining. On the first build batch the lining along the bottom of the tank and rose vertically in the middle so not following the outline of the tank. However, on the final ten it went up at the same angle as the tank as seen in the view of 84025 at Henfield on August 27, 1961.

RIGHT: One of the least photographed Standard classes were the 2MT 84XXX, based strongly on the LM Ivatt 2MT. 84020-9 formed the second batch of these engines which, with a post 1956 build date, only ever carried the second crest. A number of this batch ended up as Crewe works shunters and received unlined black as shown on 84022. The '2' power classification is carried as are electrification flashes.

BELOW RIGHT: Close inspection of Scottish Region based 4MT 80026 reveals a few differences from the previous view of 80010. Taken on August 6, 1965, we can see that this engine was once fitted with a tablet catcher and the recess cuts into the lining. The numbers are applied at 10in size and the power classification here is the extended 4MTT. Two electrification flashes are fitted to the bunker.

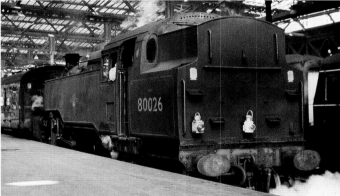

The livery of a WD should be easy - all over grime. However, unlined black did live beneath the dirt. There were variations such as the size of the numbers but 90466 was unique in carrying, incorrectly, the route restricting yellow cab stripe. Although it's difficult to be certain on this evidence, it would seem that electrification flashes had not been applied despite the date of October 1965.

RIGHT: *First of class 9F 92000 is seen at Bristol Barrow Road on August 27, 1963. With the exception of 92220 all of the 9Fs ran in unlined black with many only carrying the second crest as they were built after early 1957. However, 92000 ran with both and was also one of a small number that were modified with a double chimney, thus extra care would be needed from a modeller to get this engine right. Note that it carries the route disc but no power classification.* **T OWEN**

BELOW RIGHT: *Possibly the ultimate in lined green was the final 9F and steam engine to be built by British Railways, 92220* **Evening Star**, *seen here just days after its naming ceremony in March 1960. It had both the route and power classification markings applied. The railway press of the day reported that it was painted black on completion but was then repainted green before entering traffic.*

BELOW: *Like the WDs, the BR 9Fs were frequently covered in a layer of grime. For just a few weeks following an overhaul the unlined black livery could be seen as on Crosti rebuild 92029 at Kettering in August 1962. The power classification is carried as 9F although it is said that the Crosti engines were only regarded as an 8F. Electrification flashes are evident as are the yellow axlebox covers, in this case carrying the red stripe.* **J L CHAMPION**

A STUDY IN LIVERY VARIATIONS

At the time of building, the 82XXX class locos were given lined black livery in accordance with their 3MT power classification, carrying the small crest and showing the power classification as '3' above the number. 82001 is at Birmingham Snow Hill in July 1952. R BROUGHTON

THE BR STANDARD 82XXX TANKS

To illustrate the variations that could be encountered in liveries during this period, we finally look at one class in detail, this being the 82XXX BR Standard 2-6-2 tanks. They could be found with a host of minor livery differences, due in part to their allocation to the Western Region. As they say on the television these days, 'other variations may have existed'! ■

We also have 82000 without a numbered power classification but carrying the yellow Western Region route disc at Fairbourne in June 1961. M J READE

Following the black trail, we now see 82015 which was allocated to the Southern Region. Still with the first crest it carries the power classification 3P 2F. Full lining has been maintained.

Moving to the second crest, 82024 again has full lining but has the simple power classification of '3'. It also carries the Southern Region triangular water treatment symbol. May 4, 1963.

LEFT: *Another variation. In this image 82027, based on the North Eastern Region at the time, does not carry any power classification. The running plate lining does not go all the way to the buffer beam. This is possibly due to a paint touch up following accident damage.* **P HUGHES**

BELOW LEFT: *Whilst still in the North East, 82027 then visited Darlington works where it received large numbers. It subsequently moved to the Southern Region where the water treatment triangle will have been added to the livery. This picture was taken at Nine Elms on September 4, 1965. The running plate lining appears to have been omitted from this repaint too.* **G F BLOXHAM**

RIGHT: *The opportunities for engines to acquire lined green with the first crest were limited but some did run with the second crest in conjunction with the lining. 82001 also has both the '3' power classification and the yellow route disc at Bailey Gate on March 31, 1962.* **R PATTERSON**

BELOW: *One engine that was completely different was 82044, which whilst carrying lined black livery, had its number positioned on the cabside instead of the bunker. The lining was also omitted on the bunker.*

Turning to green, 82003 carries lined green with the first crest and a route disc at Aberystwyth in January 1962. **J LEAF**

Unlined green soon became the norm on the Western Region and was perpetuated when some engines moved to the Midland. Here 82040 has both the route disc and power classification added to the basic livery at St Philips Marsh in 1962. **P HUGHES**

Over at Dovey Junction in 1962, 82032 is again in unlined green but only has the route disc displayed.

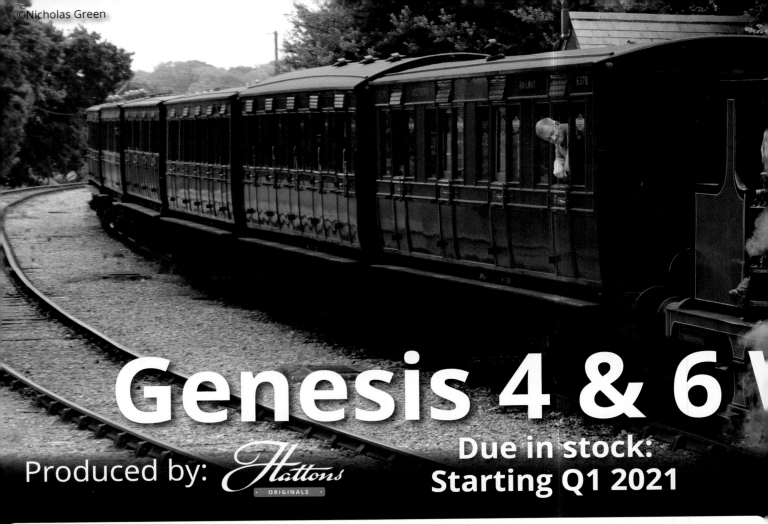

©Nicholas Green

Genesis 4 & 6 W

Produced by: *Hattons* ORIGINALS

Project Genesis faithfully represents the trains of the Era 2 & 3 (1875 - 1947) period and brings modellers the opportunity to run a detailed train of coaches in liveries not normally seen in ready-to-run form.

We are producing 7 body styles between the 4 and 6 wheel coaches. These will be used to represent a lot of different coaches when allied to the painting and printing we are applying to them.

The individual styling has been made to include the most common features from some of the most widespread and longest lasting coaches to help make them recognisable to customers.

Features

- Lit and unlit options
- Lit coaches inc. 18 pin socket
- Warm yellow LEDs in lit versions
- 7 different bodyshell variations
- 2 fully detailed underframes
- Optional lower footboards
- Full brake rigging
- Fine detailing on panelling
- Painted interiors
- Optional semi-permanent coupling
- NEM coupling pockets
- Minimum second radius

4 Wheel Coaches
Order yours online at:
www.hattons.co.uk/genesis

OO Gauge

GWR chocolate and cream

GNR lined teak

LNWR plum and spilt milk

SECR crimson lake

SR olive green

LNER pre-war brown

LMS crimson

British Railways Departmental

LBSCR mahogany

VALE OF RHEIDOL LOCOMOTIVES

We decided to give the narrow-gauge Vale of Rheidol line a page of its own because of its unique place in the history of steam locomotive liveries. The three engines, No.7, No.8 and No.9, survived all other BR steam engines and were the only ones to carry the diesel era blue livery. Indeed, the final twist in the livery story even lies outside the official scope of this book as we shall see. ■

ABOVE: *Lined green and the second crest soon followed and this picture of the nameplate of No.7 was taken in 1957.* **T OWEN**

RIGHT: *BR (diesel) blue arrived on the line before the end of mainline steam but this image dates from 1971 and shows the livery as seen on No.7* **Owain Glyndŵr.** *At least the red-backed name and number plates enlivened the livery a little.*

BELOW: *Just prior to the sale of the line in 1989 we come to the final BR steam livery. The blue has been retained but both the name and number plates have been repositioned and a metal BR arrow affixed to the cabside. The whole is set off by white lining. No.8* **Llewelyn** *and No.9* **Prince of Wales** *stand outside what was the standard gauge running shed at Aberystwyth. It was taken over when mainline steam finished operating in the area.*

The BR era started with all three engines being in black livery and un-named. The first application of green, as seen here on No.9, was in unlined form and a front number plate had not been fitted although the brackets were in place. The date is August 2, 1954. **T OWEN**

DEPARTMENTAL LIVERIES

Departmental locomotives would form an interesting subject on their own. They shunted the yards at railway works and other facilities such as a sleeper works and quarries. The Western Region did not have any official steam departmental locomotives, using already withdrawn tank engines to do the job, being replaced on a regular basis by engines that still had a few months life in them. The Midland Region was not a great fan of departmental locos either, in the main they used engines still in capital stock, for shunting duties at Crewe for example. However, the Eastern and Southern Regions had an interesting and mixed fleet employed on departmental duties. ∎

ABOVE: *Looking at the Midland Region first, departmental engines were used to shunt at Wolverton Carriage works, these being old Webb designed 'special tanks' numbered CD3 to CD7 with the latter, shown here, being the last to be withdrawn in November 1959. As can be seen in this picture taken in 1957, the first BR crest had been applied. The only other standard gauge engines were five ex Lancashire and Yorkshire Railway 0-6-0STs drawn from the large class of identical engines running in capital stock, but these carried the numbers 11304/6, 11324, 11368 and 11394 so that they could be readily identified from their capital stock comrades. Mention should also be made of the narrow gauge 0-4-0ST* Wren *that worked at Horwich.*

LEFT: *On the Southern Region a member of the small C14 class ran as 77s and is seen at Eastleigh on February 1, 1958. Honoured with lined black livery, it has the first crest and lettering for the 'Engineers Dept'.*

TOP: *Formerly 30272, G6 0-6-0T came into departmental stock in 1950 and spent ten years shunting at Meldon Quarry in Devon being numbered DS3152 for the duration. It is seen during a visit to Eastleigh works in 1954. It was painted unlined black. It was replaced at Meldon by another G6, 30238 which carried the number DS682.* T OWEN

LEFT: *A number of A1X Terriers had departmental duties but only one received a special livery for the job, this being DS377 which shunted at Brighton Works. When the works ceased carrying out BR related work in 1959 the loco was renumbered 32635 but retained the yellow livery.*

RIGHT: *Tender engines in departmental service were rare but two C class 0-6-0s were used by the Southern at Ashford works from 1962 until 1966, one of these being DS239, formerly 31592. Other than changing the cabside number it retained its BR unlined black livery with second crest from its main line days.*

BELOW LEFT: *In 1963 Ashford works had DS237 and DS238 transferred from capital stock (30065 & 30070 respectively) with them being painted in a version of the old Malachite green livery. Both were named and here we see DS238 **Wainright** before moving to Ashford, at Eastleigh in 1963. Both were withdrawn in 1967.*

The Eastern region's fleet of departmental engines was large and fluid utilising a number of classes. In this case we see Y3 Sentinel No.7 at Lowestoft. Formerly 68161, it became a departmental locomotive in March 1953 and was condemned in May 1964. In this undated picture it carries the first crest on black paint.

Another Sentinel in departmental stock was Y1 39 ex 68131. No evidence of BR ownership appears to be carried on the plain black paintwork. K FAIREY

The British Railways Steam Years From 1948

In later years, redundant USA tanks became the mainstay of the Southern's departmental fleet with six being deployed. DS233 was the first to be taken in, this being in October 1962 when it was renumbered from 30061. Although designated for working at Redbridge sleeper works, it appears to have been borrowed for some dock shunting at Southampton on June 6, 1964. Unlined black with the second crest along with Engineers' branding would suffice.

ABOVE: *A number of J50 0-6-0 tanks spent a brief time as departmental engines. Here we see the former 68914 which became No.11. All worked at Doncaster. Clearly it was decided that a good coat of paint should be applied before starting on the task which included the application of the second crest.* T OWEN

RIGHT: *Something just a little larger than the Y3 above was Y4 04-0ST 33 which used to be 68129. It spent 11 years in departmental service, all at Stratford.*

BELOW: *With the ending of the use of steam power, a number of locations that needed a supply of steam were provided with a stationary boiler in the shape of a B1 4-6-0 transferred to departmental stock. One such was 32, formerly 61315 that worked at Canklow and Barrow Hill from 1966 to 1968. The B1s carried lined black and probably all had the second crest whilst on these duties.*

One recent retiree from main line duties of those restored to traffic was D40 Gordon Highlander formerly 62277 which was withdrawn in June 1958. Here it carries Great North of Scotland Railway livery as their 49 as seen at Macduff on June 13, 1960.

THE HERITAGE FLEET

At the end of the 1950s, enthusiasts were surprised to hear that a number of vintage engines on the Scottish Region were to be restored to their former glory for use on railtours. Subsequently there was also to be one representative from each of the Midland, Southern and Western Regions. ■

BELOW RIGHT: *Restored to traffic after many years out of service was former Caledonian Railway 'single' 123. Unlike the other Scottish engines this one travelled far from home to cover railtour work and is seen at Haywards Heath on September 15, 1963.*

BELOW: *Making up the Scottish group was 256 Glen Douglas, a D34 class engine from the North British Railway. As 62469 it was in regular service until November 1959.* E RUSSELL

A startling returnee was 'Clan' goods loco 103 bedecked in Highland Railway yellow. During 1959 it was photographed at the appropriate location of Inverness. J ADAMS

ABOVE: *Moving south of the border we come to Midland Compound 1000, formerly BR 41000. This had been taken out of use in September 1951 and was to form part of the National Collection. It is seen at Sheffield.* P HUGHES

RIGHT: *T9 120 did not join the heritage party until March 1962 and remained part of capital stock whilst running in its restored form. It was formally withdrawn in July 1963, although it worked two further railtours before retirement. It also saw very occasional use on timetabled duties.* M CHAPMAN

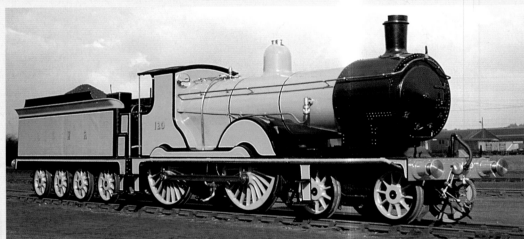

Having watched it languish in York Museum for many years, the Western Region decided to restore 3440 City of Truro to running order and it was put back into service in September 1958. Unlike the Scottish engines and 1000, when not required for railtour duty it would work service trains having regular duties to Bristol and Didcot from its Swindon base. It was withdrawn again in May 1961, a year before 30120 was painted green so there was never a time when all seven engines were in traffic together. G PARRY COLLECTION